PTE
PEARSON TEST OF ENGLISH
General

Skills Boosters
Level 4
Students' Book

PEARSON
Longman

Steve Baxter
Martyn Ellis
Susan Davies

Pearson Education Limited
Edinburgh Gate
Harlow
Essex CM20 2JE
England
and Associated Companies throughout the world.

www.pearsonlongman.com

First published 2011

ISBN: 978-1-4082-6784-4

Set in Meta Plus

Printed in Slovakia by Neografia

Acknowledgements
We are grateful to the following for permission to reproduce copyright material:

Text
Extract 1.7 adapted from "My Running Hobby Became an Obsession: A Case Study", www.runningforfun.co.uk, copyright (c) RunningForFun

In some instances we have been unable to trace the owners of copyright material, and we would appreciate any information that would enable us to do so.

The publisher would like to thank the following for their kind permission to reproduce their photographs:

(Key: b-bottom; c-centre; l-left; r-right; t-top)

Alamy Images: Martin Bond 52tl, f4foto 124b, Keith Morris 124t, Jack Sullivan 28tl, Sergiu Turcanu 106bl, Wildscape 76tr, Gari Wyn Williams 100tr; **Corbis:** Paul Burns 82tl, Roy McMahon 100tl; **iStockphoto:** 28tr, 106tl; **Pearson Free Image:** 106r; **Photolibrary.com:** Andrea Jones 52tr; **Press Association Images:** John Birdsall 82tr; **Rex Features:** OJO Images 76tl

All other images © Pearson Education

Every effort has been made to trace the copyright holders and we apologise in advance for any unintentional omissions. We would be pleased to insert the appropriate acknowledgement in any subsequent edition of this publication.

Contents

Introduction

What is the Pearson Test of English General?

PTE General is an assessment solution at six different levels of English language proficiency (A1, 1, 2, 3, 4 and 5). It tests English ability in practical skills for real-life situations such as writing messages, understanding talks, understanding newspaper and magazine articles or taking part in conversations. PTE General tests are taken four times a year in May, June, November and December in centres all around the world.
The tests do not assume any experience of work or knowledge of the world and so are most suitable for teenagers and young adults who expect to use English in their future academic and professional lives.

Key features

The sections and items in PTE General Level 4 are grouped together into themes or topics related either to global issues such as the environment, pollution, emigration, or conservation, or to more familiar matters such as work, education, travel and entertainment. The listening and reading texts are authentic and are taken from radio broadcasts, newspaper and magazine articles, telephone conversations, announcements, etc. The tests are international so the reading and listening texts are taken from a range of English-speaking countries, e.g. the UK, the USA, Australia. The four skills – listening, speaking, reading and writing – are tested in an integrated way. For example, you listen to some information and write about what you have heard, or you read a text and then answer questions or complete notes based on what you have read.

Test structure

PTE General is divided into two parts – the Written Test and the Spoken Test.

The Written Test

The Written Test of PTE General consists of nine sections and takes 2 hours and 30 minutes at Level 4.

Section 1 – Listening

Section 1 consists of ten short listening texts – dialogues or monologues. Each text is followed by a question and three possible answers. You must choose the correct answer by putting a cross (✗) in a box. There is a short pause before each recording for you to read the answers. This section tests your ability to understand the main detail of what someone says. You will hear the recording only once.

Section 2 – Listening and Writing

Section 2 is a dictation. You will hear one person speaking and you must write down exactly what you hear with the correct spelling. You hear the recording twice, the second time with pauses to give you time to write. The passage is authentic English and can be a news broadcast, an announcement, instructions or factual information.

Section 3 – Listening

In Section 3, you will hear two listening texts, including conversations, announcements and recorded messages. You have to complete a text or notes for each listening using the information you have heard. There are five gaps to fill for each listening text. This section tests your ability to understand and write down specific information. You will hear each recording only once.

Section 4 – Reading

In Section 4, you read five short texts, each containing a gap, and you choose which of three answers is the missing word or phrase that fills the gap. This section tests your ability to understand specific information and/or the overall meaning of the text. The reading texts can be instructions, signs, notices, labels, advertisements, menus or announcements.

Section 5 – Reading

Section 5 has one longer reading text. You read the text and answer five questions or complete five sentences from a choice of three answers. This section tests your understanding of the main idea of a text. The reading text can be a newspaper or magazine article, a leaflet, a brochure or a website article.

Section 6 – Reading

There are two reading texts in this section. Each text is followed by four questions for you to answer using a word or a short phrase. They test your understanding of the main points of the texts. The types of reading can be articles from newspapers or magazines, leaflets, brochures or website articles.

Section 7 – Reading

In Section 7, you read a text and use the information to fill in seven gaps in a second text or set of notes. This section tests your understanding of specific detailed information you have read. The reading text can be an advertisement, newspaper or magazine article, or a section from a website or a textbook.

Section 8 – Writing

Section 8 is a writing test. You have to write a piece of correspondence – for example an email, a formal or informal letter – based on the information that you have read in Section 7. At Level 4, you have to write 120–150 words. In your correspondence you are expected to ask for more information or to express your opinion on the subject. The topics in this section deal with global issues and current events.

Section 9 – Writing

In Section 9, you will be asked to write a text from your own experience, knowledge or imagination. The text to write at Level 4 is 200–250 words long. You will be asked to write a text which gives your point of view, explains advantages and disadvantages, or develops an argument. The text type can be an article or blog entry, a review, report or essay, or an analysis of an issue. There is a choice between two topics.

The Spoken Test

The Spoken Test of PTE General consists of four sections and takes 8 minutes at Level 4.

Section 10

In the first part of the Test, the examiner will ask you a question and you have to talk about yourself continuously for about 1.5 minutes. You may talk about your interests, hobbies, the sports you take part in, the films or books you like, or about things you have done in the past. The examiner will ask you further questions to find out more information. The whole section is 2 minutes in length.

Section 11

In Section 11, you will be asked to give your opinions and ideas about a subject suggested by the examiner and to support your ideas. The examiner will take the opposite point of view for the discussion. The topics will include subjects of everyday interest, for example, the advantages of mobile phones, fast food, living in the city or in the country, or more general subjects such as pollution or emigration. The discussion will be for about 2 minutes.

Section 12

In Section 12, you will be shown two pictures and asked to describe them. First, you will be asked to compare and contrast the pictures and then you will be asked to interpret one aspect of them. You will have about 2 minutes to do this.

Section 13

The final section of the Spoken Test is a role play. You will be given a card with details of your role, a situation and some instructions. The situation usually contains a problem which you have to solve by talking to the examiner, or a course of action that you have to explain and justify. This section of the Test takes about 2 minutes.

PTE General Skills Boosters

The *PTE General Skills Boosters* have been specially written to help you become familiar with the format and content of the PTE General Test. They contain five full practice tests, plus language and skills development sections in each unit to help you to improve your general level of English as well as your score in the test. Each level of the *PTE General Skills Boosters* contains:

- Five Practice Tests for both the Written and Spoken Tests, with Tips giving advice on how to approach each section and deal with particular problems that might occur.
- Vocabulary and Grammar practice sections which focus on the language linked to the themes of the tests.
- Skills development sections to practise each of the four skills in the tests – listening, speaking, reading and writing.
- A Writing guide which concentrates on the writing tasks you will meet in the tests, giving example answers, writing tips and practice questions.
- A Glossary with those words and phrases in the tests that you may need help with. Each item is followed by a definition.

Unit One

The themes for this unit are: music/work/health and fitness/relationships

Vocabulary and Grammar

Vocabulary 1: Collocation

Match each word on the left with one from the right and then complete the sentences that follow, as in the example.

employment	~~range~~
labour	profession
strict	expectancy
status	market
natural	skills
~~broad~~	loss
eating	symbol
weight	disorder
life	history
organising	diet
vocational	progression

Example: The store stocked a ..*broad range*.. of classical music scores.

1 Throughout her teens she suffered from a debilitating .... brought on by the stresses and strains of her young life.

2 Local authorities are concerned at the cost of caring for the elderly as .... continues to rise.

3 When he was no longer able to play the game he loved, it seemed a .... to move into management.

4 He was always likely to go into a .... like teaching or social work.

5 One thing is for sure – the size of the .... for graduates is decreasing as more qualified people seek fewer openings.

6 Contrary to what many people believe, ... need not be difficult, so long as you plan your eating carefully.

7 After the operation, he was placed on a .... of fresh fruit and vegetables.

8 These new environmentally friendly cars are also becoming a .... amongst the middle classes.

9 He became a successful manager because his .... made the work of those around him much easier.

10 When creating your CV for a job application, it is vital that you include full details of your ....

Vocabulary 2: Idiomatic and figurative language

Match each of the following with its meaning and then use the verb expressions <u>in the correct form</u> to complete the sentences, as in the example.

1	~~to take stock~~	**a**	to initiate
2	to open the door to	**b**	to be worth the effort
3	to bring tears to the eyes	**c**	to make progress
4	to catch up with	**d**	to be in good condition mentally and physically
5	to pick up	**e**	to succeed in the face of difficulty
6	to come to a head	**f**	~~to consider the implications~~
7	to feel on top of the world	**g**	to get up to date with something
8	to pay off	**h**	make available
9	to trigger	**i**	to acquire
10	to get somewhere	**j**	to cause to become emotional
11	to come through	**k**	to reach a critical stage

Example: Having to take time off work following her accident gave Louise time _to take stock_ of her stressful schedule.

1 His new position of influence within the company .... many useful new contacts.

2 The dramatic scene where the woman is forced to decide which child to save reminded John of his own experience and ....

3 When he goes on holiday, he doesn't relax; he uses the time .... his work.

4 Working with young children meant he was always likely .... several coughs and colds over the year.

5 Joe's uneasy relationship with his demanding boss .... when he was asked to work at the weekend at very short notice.

6 After three weeks off lazing around in a sunny climate, Jane .... by the end of her holiday.

7 The extra training he put himself through after the injury obviously .... as he was ready for the new season.

8 Robert's chance remark .... a sequence of events that ended in tragedy.

9 With the latest results looking so positive, we realised that we were .... and would be crazy to stop the experiments now.

10 There were moments along the way when he felt he couldn't go on, but he .... in the end.

Vocabulary 3: Words with more than one meaning

Use each of the words in the box twice to fill the gaps in the sentences, as in the example. Change the form of the word if necessary.

~~pursuit~~ arrangement pressure vehicle development movement

Example: He worked hard all week but at the weekend engaged in a number of outdoor ..pursuits.. .
The thief rushed out of the apartment block, with the police in ..pursuit.. .

1 They decided to take a break from each other for a few weeks and at first the .... worked well.

2 It was a windy day, and the constant .... of the boat in the choppy sea made him feel sick.

3 He was very talented and had lots of ideas, but in the end the .... of constant deadlines got the better of him.

4 All the .... have been made for the wedding. We just have to hope for good weather now.

5 The novel is a thinly disguised .... for his political views.

6 A faulty valve had allowed the .... to build up in the boiler, causing it to explode.

7 The police had all but given up their search for the missing man, when an unexpected .... revitalised the investigation.

8 But it is ironically in the slow .... of this stunning symphony that the music suddenly comes alive.

9 The area is of course very different now as a result of widespread urban ....

10 This is the only .... which can negotiate this kind of rough terrain.

Grammar 1: Linking words

Choose the correct option to complete each sentence, as in the example.

Example: You may not be completely successful, ..but.. it's important you show a willingness to help.
 (A) but **B** and **C** because

1 I think I have my approach all worked out now, ... strategically but emotionally, too.
 A not really **B** not so **C** not just

2 .... it's possible to over-exercise, not exercising at all is much worse.
 A Because **B** Whenever **C** Although

3 He only agreed to the proposal in principle .... it allowed him to buy some time to think it over.
 A however **B** because **C** before

4 At work he was known throughout the office for his fierce temper, ... at home he was a loving husband and father.
 A so **B** yet **C** and

5 .... planning the next multi-million pound company project or a weekend away with his family, he would employ the same attention to detail.
 A Whether **B** Although **C** Despite

6 .... he sits around all day and does no exercise, he is as thin as a rake.

   A Though   **B** When   **C** Whereas

7 The hospital was severely criticised in the report .... its poor hygiene record.

   A owing to   **B** despite   **C** as well as

8 .... the manager is a demanding leader, his staff are full of respect for him.

   A Whereas   **B** When   **C** While

9 .... we should always show respect to those around us, so we should expect those around us to show us the same respect.

   A Although   **B** Just as   **C** Whenever

10 The doctor says James is well enough to go back to work, ... he will have to take it easy for the first few weeks.

   A but   **B** and   **C** so

Grammar 2: Passives

Change these active sentences into the passive form, as in the example.

Example: Your employers won't pay you any more, even if you work harder.

       You won't _be paid any more (by your employers), even if you work harder_ .

1 Sometimes I think that my employees don't appreciate my work.

   Sometimes I think my work ....

2 When you challenge him about the standard of his work, he makes lots of excuses.

   When he ....

3 The media have rightly criticised him for his poor performances in recent films.

   He has ....

4 You should always treat serious musicians with respect.

   Serious musicians ....

5 I think we should encourage the fact that he is playing in a rock band, not criticise it.

   The fact ....

6 Some health officials consider this kind of treatment to be a waste of hospital resources.

   This kind of treatment ....

7 His frequent health problems certainly affected our relationship.

   Our relationship ....

8 My illness forced me to think seriously about the damage I was doing to my body.

   I ....

9 When I got back to work, someone had moved all my stuff to another office.

   When I got back to work, all my stuff ....

10 I'm sure one of the officers would have assisted the man if he had asked.

   I'm sure the man ....

Grammar 3: Functions and reporting verbs

Rewrite the information in the sentences in reported form using verbs from the box, as in the example.

~~warn~~   report   announce   recommend   demand
thank   complain   advise (x2)   praise   offer

Example: "Look Joe. You'd better get the job done today because you know what the boss is like."
.. He warned Joe to get the job done .. .

1   "I don't think you should work so hard, Jane."
Max ....

2   "We will be increasing production of the new model."
A spokesman for the company ....
....

3   "We can play the song again for you if you like."
The band leader ....

4   "It's very good of you to invite me, Ann."
He ....

5   "Jack, if that's the way you feel, you should find another job."
Jack's wife ....

6   "Well Mr Smith, I think this is the best diet for someone in your condition."
The doctor ....

7   "I'm very proud of him because he worked so hard to get where he is today."
The trainer ....

8   "We can now use science to observe what happens to the brain while we are listening to music."
The correspondent ....
....

9   "I'm really not happy with the amount of work we are being given to do."
He ....

10   "Mike, I need you to finish the report by tomorrow; leave everything else and do it now."
The manager ....
....

Language skills

● Listening 1: Listen for gist and specific information

Listen to the recording. Which of the three options is the best summary?
Options:

1   People who enjoy their work are understandably happy because on average we spend about a third of our lives at work; that's a long time if you are not happy.

2   Most of us enjoy our jobs because we are lucky to have one and it helps us to pay for the things we need. We have plenty of time to relax.

3 There are probably more people who like their jobs than those who don't, but these are the ones who have the good fortune to have a job in the first place.

◉ Listening 2: Making notes

Listen to this radio item about health clubs and complete the notes that follow.

1 People who benefit most from the fitness industry: ....

2 A cheaper option to keep fit: ....

3 What fitness clubs offer: ....

4 What the experts help you to do: ....

5 The real reason people go to fitness clubs: ....

6 What fitness club members believe about themselves: ....

7 What lots of gym members find: ....

8 Why gym members rarely cancel membership: ....

Writing: Sentence transformation

Read the sentences below. Rewrite them as more complex sentences beginning with the words shown, as in the example.

Example: He spent time in hospital. You should not talk to him about this.

      One thing *you should not talk to him about is the time he spent in hospital* .

1 There is only one way to make him look for a job. That is to stop his allowance.
The only ....
....

2 He didn't tell anyone about the fact that he had a part-time job. This was very surprising.
What ....
....

3 He intended to leave the band. He announced this at the last minute.
Only ....
....

4 Many people find the lack of immediate physical improvement discouraging. This is what makes them give up their programme of exercise.
It's ....
....

5 He has the project he is working on. He has no further work planned until the New Year. This is a problem.
The problem is that, ...
....

Practice Test One

Section 1

You will have 10 seconds to read each question and the corresponding options. Then listen to the recording. After the recording you will have 10 seconds to choose the correct option. Put a cross (X) in the box next to the correct answer, as in the example.

Example: What aspect of customer service is the speaker talking about?
A [X] dealing with customers by telephone
B ☐ dealing with customers in a store
C ☐ dealing with customers in their homes

1. What do we learn about Mike?
   A ☐ He wants the report by the end of the week.
   B ☐ He doesn't mind if the report is a bit late.
   C ☐ He expects the report at the agreed time.

2. What is David's attitude towards work?
   A ☐ Do more than you have to.
   B ☐ Do as much as you have to do.
   C ☐ Do as little as possible.

3. Who is the speaker?
   A ☐ a local radio newsreader
   B ☐ a local factory manager
   C ☐ a local person looking for work

4. Who are the two speakers?
   A ☐ two members of a music band
   B ☐ a band member and his manager
   C ☐ a band member and a reporter

5. What is the speaker talking about?
   A ☐ the quality of a recorded piece of music
   B ☐ the progression of a piece of music
   C ☐ a live performance of a piece of music

6. How does the man feel?

A ☐ pleasantly surprised

B ☐ as he expected

C ☐ relieved the woman liked it

7. How does Jack feel about exercising?

A ☐ It requires a lot of concentration.

B ☐ It has not been difficult.

C ☐ It has had an unexpected result.

8. What is the speaker doing?

A ☐ advising

B ☐ threatening

C ☐ encouraging

9. Where is the speaker?

A ☐ in a radio studio

B ☐ in a lecture theatre

C ☐ in a doctor's consultation room

10. Who is the speaker referring to?

A ☐ a boxer

B ☐ an athlete

C ☐ a footballer

Test Tip

Remember that you have only one chance to listen, so be sure to read the question or sentence beginning. Listen out for the tone and the intonation, and make full use of the pauses so that you are ready to choose the answer. For example, in Question 8, reading the choices should prepare you to listen out for the tone of the woman's voice alongside the language she uses to arrive at the right answer.

Section 2

You will hear a recording about the effect of changing employment patterns on retirement. Listen to the whole recording once. Then you will hear the recording again with pauses for you to write down what you hear. Make sure you spell the words correctly.

11.

Test Tip

If what you have written down doesn't make grammatical or logical sense, then you have probably misheard it, so consider changing it to something that sounds similar and makes sense.

Section 3

 You will hear a radio interview with a scientist talking about why music makes us happy. First, read the notes below, then listen and complete the notes with information from the interview.

Example: The iPod has made music much more *accessible/available* .

---

12   We can analyse the emotional effects of music because of advancements in ....

13   Music is used by babies to communicate ....

14   Sound patterns give us pleasure because they are ....

15   When we hear a rhythm, the bloodstream is filled with ....

16   Music helps us to ....

Test Tip

In note-completion exercises, the notes immediately before the gap are often written in a different way to what you hear in the text. When listening for the relevant information, it is important to recognise this. For example, in Question 15, where you hear "causes the release of chemicals into the bloodstream", you read "the bloodstream is filled with _____".

 You will hear a radio presentation about people's attitudes to work. First, read the notes below, then listen and complete the notes with information from the presentation.

The same people who complain about work would hate to (**Example:**) *lose their jobs*. All jobs have

their 17 .... , but some things have to be done. Some people feel

they are not 18 .... or complain about their companies. People who

seem to enjoy their jobs tend to be in 19 .... Modern

living has made some people unable to deal with 20 .... This

type of person would be no different if they 21 ....

Section 4

Read each text and put a cross (X) by the missing word or phrase, as in the example.

Example:

> Whether you're looking for your very first job, switching careers, or re-entering the job market after .... , finding a job whittles down to two main tasks: understanding yourself and understanding the job market.

A   ☒   an extended absence
B   ☐   a short holiday
C   ☐   an application

22.

> PAY THE BILLS, BUY THE GROCERIES, OWN A HOME.
> *Get work, make money. Anyone can find a job to do.*
> *But finding a job to love is ....*
> FIND GREAT SELF-EMPLOYMENT JOBS.

A   ☐   all you need
B   ☐   another matter
C   ☐   just as easy

23.

> Though it was probably one of the most audacious debuts in rock history and quickly established him as one of the premier songwriters of his generation, Elvis Costello's *My Aim is True* has always felt more like a demonstration disc than a recording intended for ....

A   ☐   rehearsal purposes
B   ☐   national consumption
C   ☐   commercial release

24.

Within the musical structure of 12-bar blues, there is elegant simplicity. Yet enormous variety can be applied to that structure. Mastery of the art can take a lifetime, but we can teach you .... in a very short time. Classes start June 5ᵗʰ.

A ☐ the guitar

B ☐ the basics

C ☐ everything

25.

Did you know? For the first time since the Civil War, American life expectancy will soon decrease, owing to the diseases associated with obesity. Dr Michael Fuchs, eminent nutritionist, will be talking about how to .... obesity in Tuesday's lunchtime lecture.

A ☐ avoid

B ☐ help

C ☐ disable

26.

NOTICE

This fitness centre will be closed for four days
from 11ᵗʰ to 14ᵗʰ March
whilst we install
new state-of-the-art equipment.
We look forward to .... our members back
to our improved facilities.
Thanks for your patience.

A ☐ inviting

B ☐ getting

C ☐ welcoming

Read the passage and complete the sentences below. Put a cross (X) in the box next to the correct answer, as in the example.

Don't let WORK RULE YOUR LIFE

Maybe a short holiday is a good time to reflect on how much your working life is taking out of your real life. Most of us would accept that work is an essential pursuit for the obvious reasons of making a living, but also to provide us with a more rounded lifestyle. But employment has extended itself into our lives so much that we may question the level of satisfaction it brings. Why should this be?

Take advances in technology, for example. On the plus side, computerisation can provide freedom and different options in the workplace. Working by computer from home, for example, has enabled many workers to combine family responsibilities with a full-time job.

But just as technology can bring these kinds of advantages to our work, it can also increase the amount of time spent at work. Gone are the days when finishing work meant finishing work, if you see what I mean, as we can now take our work home with us thanks to mobile phones, PCs and email facilities. Technology can be a wonderful help to us, but only if directed in ways to improve and simplify, not complicate and add stress.

Interestingly, some of the more progressive organisations have actually brought the home to work, providing facilities for children in order to ease the pressure on working mums and dads.

Unfortunately, the opposite may occur, with the same mums and dads feeling they have no excuse to go home and so staying that bit longer.

While enjoying the advantages that technology and alternate work arrangements can provide, we should also take a look at the way our approach to work has an effect on everything we do at home. It now seems very important to be busy at almost anything all the time. Being busy seems to have become a good thing, no matter what you are doing. Busy-ness (as opposed to business) is good; thinking and reflecting on your life is bad. Speed is praised; deliberation is not.

Too much emphasis on always staying late, always working, always "doing" at the expense of "being" can lead to serious health problems, as well as feelings of alienation. It has never been more important to clarify our needs, and to spend time in a way that reflects the important aspects of our lives.

Example: Apart from earning a living, what should work provide?

A ☐ holidays
B ☒ satisfaction
C ☐ lifestyle

27. What has technology brought to the workplace?
A ☐ flexibility in the way we work
B ☐ increased job satisfaction
C ☐ more relaxed working conditions

28. What is the result of increased access to technology at work?
A ☐ People become lazy.
B ☐ People work ineffectively.
C ☐ People work more hours.

29. What happens when companies offer family facilities at work?
A ☐ Kids don't want to go home.
B ☐ The parents relax more.
C ☐ The parents work till later.

30. What is beginning to influence home life?
A ☐ the way we are encouraged to work
B ☐ access to much more leisure time
C ☐ the constant use of technology

31. Which of the following is the author's message?
A ☐ Don't take your work home.
B ☐ Establish your priorities.
C ☐ Use technology to your advantage.

Test Tip

For this section, make sure you look at the questions and see if there are any you can answer easily. If you can get two or three of them to begin with, it will make you more confident for the others.

Section 6

Read the article below and answer the questions, as in the example.

I HAVE TWO DAUGHTERS TO WHOM MUSIC MEANS TWO VERY DIFFERENT THINGS. To the elder, music is simply there, a poorly reproduced background accompaniment to her life that stays in the background while she gets breakfast or dresses for an evening out. Music wakes her up in the morning and sends her to sleep at night. To her, music is secondary to the important things in life, a catchy tune accompanied by forgettable commentary.

My younger daughter has a completely different approach. For her, music should be treated with respect. The artist's efforts, from inception to production, deserve our full attention. Just as we sit down to watch a film, then we should sit down to listen to music, maybe a whole album, CD, download, in whatever form you like. Admire the lyrics, the instrumental expertise, the vocals, the production values.
In a world of surround sound, of MTV, of iPods, of supermarkets and shopping malls, music is everywhere, but it's nowhere, and it's killing the art of listening.

Example: How does the writer describe the role of music in his elder daughter's life?
a background accompaniment

32. What does the writer imply his elder daughter doesn't do when she has music on?

....

33. What phrase is used to describe the contribution of music radio presenters?

....

34. What other art form seems to be more respected than music?

....

35. What is affected by music being "everywhere"?

....

Section 6 Continued

Read the article below and answer the questions, as in the example.

*L*earning music is a bit like learning a language: there is a natural progression in development. Exposing children from an early age to a broad range of music, with its varying tones and pitches, will enable them to distinguish differences in music, much as infants acquire the ability to distinguish their parents' native language from a foreign language. As children develop muscle coordination and a sense of rhythm between the ages of three and five, they should be encouraged to sing along to music and engage in rhythmic activities, such as clapping, swinging, dancing, tapping, marching, and using non-melodic instruments such as drums and cymbals. As the ability to recognize and imitate rhythm develops, starting at around the age of four, children can begin to accompany singing with melodic instruments. Although certain stages in child development are considered sensitive for developing specific musical and spatial abilities, no one blueprint will help your child become a master musician.

Example: What do learning music and learning a language have in common?
   natural progression

36. What differentiates styles of music?

....

37. What physical quality enables young children to accompany music?

....

38. What do children learn to appreciate as their musical awareness develops?

....

39. What is the best plan to ensure your child becomes a good musician?

....

Read the article below and complete the sentences that follow. Write no more than three words in each gap.

My Running Hobby
Became an Obsession

I was bitten by the running bug while still at school. The thrill of competition against others, but mostly against myself, became my main focus in life. But when my relationships started to be adversely affected and my weight began to plummet, I was forced to take a fresh look at my running.

I was convinced that the only way to improve my fitness was to run further than the previous week. I was getting up at the crack of dawn to run before work, and I was going for a long run after work; it was the same at the weekends. I even started to take time off work if I was unable to run just so I could catch up with my running, if I had missed a session. Of course, looking back now I can see that it had become completely ridiculous, but at the time I was blinded by the obsession. There was just enough time for me to eat, work and sleep, but the rest of my life was taken up by running. I was spending very little time with my boyfriend and our relationship started to suffer.

I went too far. I started to pick up a lot of niggling injuries and I was fatigued by overtraining. Rather than take the rest my body was crying out for, I ploughed on and so never got the chance to recover from my injuries.

People at work started to notice that I was losing weight, but as I wasn't heavy in the first place, people were concerned rather than complimentary. I'm sure they thought I had a serious illness or an eating disorder. The problem was that, although I was eating healthy foods, my calorie intake was insufficient to maintain the required balance, if I was doing all that running.

The weight loss worried my boyfriend and the whole running obsession came to a head when he temporarily walked out on me. As far as he was concerned, it was the only way. It was the jolt I needed, because it made me look at my life and realise I was destroying myself.

I took a complete break from running and concentrated on fixing the friendships that had suffered because of my obsession. I also got my boyfriend back.

It's amazing how the body can recover so quickly. I was over my injuries in no time and soon back to my usual weight. I've started to run again, but there are always strict limits on the amount of time I dedicate to my hobby. If I overstep the mark, my boyfriend is quick to point me in the right direction again.

Example: Although she entered races against other people, the writer herself provided her main competition.

40. The first physical problems the writer noticed concerned her ....

41. If she missed a running session, she felt obliged to ....

42. As well as her physical condition, dedication to her "hobby" adversely affected her

....

43. When she experienced tiredness and injury she ....

44. People at work may have thought she was ....

45. She only became fully aware of her problems when ....

46. Nowadays, in her running she is careful not to ....

Test Tip
Paraphrasing: linking words and phrases. Learn to identify clues to where to find the answers. For example, in Question 42, you'll see "as well as her physical condition ..." and this is followed at the end of the phrase by "adversely affect". So you are looking for another negative reference in the text apart from references to her poor health.

Section 8

Use information from Section 7 to help you write your answer.

> **Test Tip**
> *Make sure that you include all the information required by the bullet points, otherwise you risk losing marks, however good the English is.*

47. **You have read the article about an obsession with running. Write an article for a magazine about the dangers of over-exercising. Write about 120–150 words. In your article you should:**
    - briefly discuss the benefits of leading a healthy lifestyle
    - describe the danger signs of overdoing the exercise
    - describe ways of ensuring you do not become over-obsessed by exercise

Write your answer here. Do not write outside the box.

Section 9

 Choose one of the topics below and write your answer in 200–250 words.

48. A) Employment and work

You see the following entry in a magazine.

> *"All work and no play makes Jack a dull boy."*
>
> Experts are always telling us that we should try to achieve a balance between our working lives and our leisure time, but very few suggest ways of doing this.
>
> WE INVITE YOUR IDEAS.

Write a response to the magazine describing your own ideas on this topic.

Or

48. B) Music

Write an essay entitled "Other People's Music".
Include the following:

- The type of music that annoys you.
- The places and circumstances where you would rather not listen to music.
- How you can avoid the annoyance of unwanted music.

Write your answer here. Do not write outside the box.

Section 10 (2 minutes)

In this section you will speak on your own for about a minute and a half. Listen to what your teacher/examiner asks. Your teacher/examiner will ask one of the main questions below and ask the follow-up questions if necessary.

Main prompt 1:
- When you were young did you have dreams of what you wanted to do as a career? What were they?

Follow-up prompts:
- What kind of advice did you get at school in terms of career?
- How did your parents influence you in deciding what to do in your life?
- What advice would you give to young people about how to decide on their future careers?
- What do you think are the main barriers to young people achieving their dreams?

Main prompt 2:
- How important is music in your life?

Follow-up prompts:
- How has your taste in music changed over the years?
- What for you are the main differences between listening to live music and recorded music?
- Why do you think music is so important to young people?
- How much does fashion dictate taste in music?

Main prompt 3:
- What aspects of your life are concerned with health and fitness?

Follow-up prompts:
- How do you think your generation is different from previous generations in terms of health and fitness?
- In what ways does modern life make it more difficult to keep healthy?
- How do any of your friends behave in ways that make them unhealthy?
- How far do you think your genes dictate how healthy you are?

Main prompt 4:
- How important is it for you to keep contact with your friends?

Follow-up prompts:
- Have you kept friends from your childhood? (Why? Why not?)
- How do you think men and women treat friendships differently?
- What needs do your friends fulfil?
- How difficult is it to keep friends who have moved away?

Test Tip

You may need thinking time to give an answer to the given question. You can give yourself such time by techniques such as paraphrasing the question: "So what did I dream about doing when I was young?" You can also use expressions to give yourself time without stopping speaking. For example: "Let me think …, I don't remember anything in particular, but …, I don't think I thought about my future life much when I was young."

Section 11 (2 minutes)

In this section you will discuss something with your teacher/examiner.

Are people nowadays too concerned with their diet and their appearance?

What do you think?

Your teacher/examiner will use the following arguments to take an opposing view to yours.

For people being too concerned:	• We should all learn to relax and enjoy life more. • It's your character that counts, not how you look. • Worrying about your appearance is actually unhealthy. • Most diets don't actually work in the long term.

Against people being too concerned:	• There are good reasons why we should take care of our health. • More and more people nowadays are overweight. • People are more confident when they feel good about themselves. • It's better to be too concerned than not at all.

Test Tip

If you are not sure what the question means exactly, use the fact that this section is a discussion to question the examiner. This will allow you to establish an agreed meaning.

Section 12 (2 minutes)

In this section you will talk for up to 1 minute about two pictures showing ways to learn about different cultures through making online friends. The pictures are being considered for a website. Tell your teacher/examiner what you can see in the pictures.

Your teacher/examiner will now put this secondary prompt.

Which picture would you choose for the website? Why?

> **Test Tip**
>
> *There are two parts to this section: to describe the pictures and to compare and contrast them to fit a given purpose. You may have forgotten the given purpose when you get to this part. Ask the examiner to remind you: "Sorry, could you just tell me again what the pictures are to be used for?"*

Section 13 (2 minutes)

In this section you will take part in a role play with your teacher/examiner. Here is a card with the situation and your goal.

TEST TAKER'S CARD	
The situation:	You and a friend have had an argument and are not speaking to each other. You are talking to another friend who knows you both.
Your goal:	Explain why you are angry and why your friend should apologise.

You are at work. Your teacher/examiner is the person who knows you both. Below is a sample script that your teacher/examiner may use.

Ready? You start.

I hear you and Lee are not talking to each other.

What's it all about?

It doesn't really matter whose fault it was, does it?

You two have been friends for ages.

You can't go on like this forever.

Someone has to make the first move.

That is the end of the test.

Unit Two

The themes for this unit are: politics/literature/emotions/local, national and global issues

Vocabulary and Grammar

Vocabulary 1: Collocation – verbs and nouns

Complete the following sentences with a verb from the list below, as in the example. Make sure you use the correct form of the verb.

raise   ~~reach~~   burst into   show   lose   give   run   meet   strike   keep   realise

Example: After six months working in such difficult conditions, he had .._reached_.. the limit of his endurance.

1 When her favourite cat went missing, she was very upset and frequently .... tears for days afterwards.
2 Throughout the novel, the author is obviously .... an opinion about what he thinks is wrong with the world.
3 Many politicians think we should .... taxes in order to pay for the extra expenditure.
4 After his early success, he failed to .... his potential as a great writer.
5 There was always an unpleasant atmosphere in the office as the boss was always .... his temper with his staff.
6 Doctors felt that the man's breakdown was partly attributable to the fact that he never .... his emotions as a child.
7 He said the literary prize money would go to a good cause and he .... his promise by giving it to a special charity.
8 After the huge success of their first album, the band's follow-up offering failed to .... expectations.
9 She either gets over-enthusiastic about life or terribly depressed; she needs to .... a balance in her emotions.
10 If he writes another complicated, impenetrable novel, he .... the risk of alienating his fans.

Vocabulary 2: Collocation – adjectives and nouns

Complete the following texts with an adjective from the list below, as in the example.

~~thorough~~   lasting   fundamental   bursting   political   emotional
bygone   universal   uncontrollable   institutional   missing

Text 1
The first thing the new president will do is to carry out a (**Example:**) .._thorough_.. analysis of the financial records of the last few years in an attempt to discover the extent of the

1 .... corruption which has stained the character of the party. Of course, the
2 .... agenda behind this move is to help to build trust amongst the electorate.
"My predecessors may have been corrupt," he is saying, "but we see gaining the trust of the people
as a 3 .... issue."

Text 2

His more recent novels have a 4 .... appeal, in direct contrast to the rather
dark and inward-looking early works which, although well-written and likely to bring him
5 .... recognition in the literary world, were a challenge for even his most
avid readers. These later, more populist works, usually set in a 6 .... age, full
of colour, costume and conflict, are likely to earn him millions through film rights as offers from
producers start to pour in. It seems that the 7 .... ingredient of his earlier
novels was a bit of action!

Text 3

He would never think about a suggestion calmly and logically before giving his answer. He was
far more likely to provide an ill-considered 8 .... response, which was
guaranteed to make the conversation escalate into another disagreement, culminating in him
reaching 9 .... point, which caused him to storm violently out of the room in
a crazy, 10 .... rage.

Vocabulary 3: Idiomatic and figurative expressions

Replace each underlined phrase in the sentences with an idiomatic phrase from the box, as in the example. In some cases you will have to change the form of the idiomatic expression.

> stand up for oneself   live up to one's promise   through thick and thin   open doors
> a bygone age   take a back seat   under the surface   fall prey to   ~~make the most of~~
> sweep something under the carpet   fly off the handle

Example: With none of the financial backing enjoyed by his opponents, Joe James mounted a
successful political campaign by <u>making full use of</u> his limited resources.
making the most of

1 The sensitive issue of the politician's previous life was <u>covered up to avoid it becoming public</u>.

....

2 She was a model student and a high achiever, but frequently <u>became the victim of</u> her emotions
as she found it difficult to handle the pressure. ....

3 His behaviour was very unpredictable and he was likely to <u>become very angry at any moment</u> if
things weren't going well. ....

4 Although they experienced difficulties during their long life together, they stuck together <u>in good
times and bad times</u>. ....

5 As he approached retirement age, he began to <u>let others take a more active role</u> during the more
vigorous promotion campaigns. ....

6 He had always been the weak one at school, but as a result of his therapy he learned to <u>be strong
and not allow others to push him around</u>. ....

7 No-one ever saw him; he was the product of <u>another time</u>, living with the barest necessities and with none of the comforts of modern life. ....

8 His early essays at school showed that he would have a great future as a novelist and he certainly <u>met expectations</u>. ....

9 He gives the impression of being friendly but, <u>despite appearances</u>, he's a ruthless political operator. ....

10 The literary prize didn't offer much financial reward, but winning it certainly <u>gave opportunities he wouldn't otherwise have had</u>. ....

Grammar 1: Reporting and rephrasing

Rewrite the sentences, using verbs from the box in the correct form and changing any other parts of the sentence that need to be changed, as in the example.

decline insint claim recommend criticise ~~realise~~
question accuse report apologise refuse

Example: "Oh, so it's Jack's brother who is running for election. I had no idea," said John.
    John didn't realise it was Jack's brother who was running for election.

1 "It's a book I think all our listeners will find fascinating," said the presenter.

....

2 "I have to get the results by Friday at the latest," she said.

....

3 "Look, I don't want to talk about the matter any more," he said.

....

4 "I'm afraid I am not at liberty to respond to that question at the moment," said the minister.

....

5 "I must admit I find his decision to stop writing the kind of books for which he is so famous as rather unusual," said the agent.

....

....

6 "Don't lie, I know it was you who took the book; I saw you do it," she said.

....

7 "Having looked very carefully at the facts in this case, I can only conclude that everything possible was done to avoid the accident."

....

8 "It is my belief that Marcia's breakdown was caused by the terrible treatment she received from her employers," said the lawyer.

....

....

9 "The whole political system functions poorly," he said.

....

10 "I would just like to say that I am very sorry for any distress I may have caused as a result of my actions," she said.

....

Grammar 2: Passive and active sentences

Change each of the following sentences from the active to the passive form, as in the example.

Example: He wrote his greatest works during the most difficult period of his life.

His greatest works were written during the most difficult period of his life.

1   I've asked you the same question three times and you have not given me an answer.

....

....

2   We need to discuss these issues and have to bring the facts to the attention of the public.

....

....

3   Having made that point, we have to accept that we are just as accountable to the country as anyone else in public office.

....

....

4   They intended to produce better-educated young people throughout the country by raising the school-leaving age.

....

....

5   Great works of literature affect us deeply and emotionally because they integrate themes that are common to us all.

....

....

6   The interviewer put the man under great pressure during the programme and asked him some provocative questions.

....

....

7   People have always believed that life in the corridors of power is corrupt.

....

....

8   Because my parents brought me up as an only child, I had lots of time by myself, which was when they introduced me to books of all kinds.

....

....

9   I must admit any kind of politics bores me and great literature interests me much more.

....

....

10 She is very excited because they are presenting her with a special prize for the progress she has made at school.

....

....

Language skills

⊙ Listening: Key words

Listen to the recording and write down key words which carry the main information. There are pauses to allow you to do this. The first one is done as an example.

Example: politicians – votes – new voters

1 ....

2 ....

3 ....

4 ....

5 ....

6 ....

7 ....

⊙ Speaking and listening: Disagreeing

Listen to the discussion on help to poorer countries. Note down the words and phrases used by the speakers to question or counter any ideas. For example: *Surely you agree ...*

1 ....

2 ....

3 ....

4 ....

5 ....

6 ....

Find a partner and practise using questions and counter arguments to discuss this question:

Do governments and individuals in the developed world have a responsibility to give aid to the less developed world?

If possible, record yourselves and check how well you have used the expressions.

Writing: Sequencing

Rewrite the following sentences and phrases in the right sequence. The first sentence does not change position. Use the <u>underlined</u> words to help you. There may be more than one possibility.

Example: We hear a lot from opposition politicians about what they are going to do when they get into power.

> **A** I don't think there is any point to <u>this</u>.
>
> **B** <u>But</u> when they get the power, I'm not sure that they do anything different.
>
> **C** <u>In fact</u>, they seem to get very quiet and it's the turn of the other party to start criticising.
>
> **D** We <u>also</u> hear a lot about what the current government is doing wrong.
>
> Key: D, B, C, A

1 Choosing what to read on holiday is one of the biggest decisions we have to make as we pack our cases every summer.

> **A** <u>It's</u> a difficult decision.
>
> **B** <u>It's one</u> you won't be able to make again until the following year.
>
> **C** <u>Or</u> perhaps a popular undemanding crime novel.
>
> **D** Should you take a classic piece of literature?

2 Some people like a good old-fashioned cry in the cinema, and that's why the classic 'tear jerker' is still so popular amongst filmgoers.

> **A** Surely enough of our lives are <u>miserable enough</u> already.
>
> **B** <u>So</u> what motivates people to get <u>even more miserable</u> in their free time?
>
> **C** There is obviously a point to getting emotional in the cinema.
>
> **D** <u>But</u> I'm not sure exactly what <u>it</u> is.

3 I was reading the other day about a husband-and-wife team of politicians who somehow manage to balance a busy family life with terribly demanding jobs in government.

> **A** Or perhaps they're just very well-organised.
>
> **B** I don't know how they do it.
>
> **C** They must be superhuman.
>
> **D** As someone whose only desire after a day's work is to relax, I am full of admiration.

Practice Test Two

Section 1

 You will have 10 seconds to read each question and the corresponding options. Then listen to the recording. After the recording you will have 10 seconds to choose the correct option. Put a cross (X) in the box next to the correct answer, as in the example.

Example: What is the speaker's message?

A   [X]   Some people lie to get what they want.

B   ☐   It's important to make popular decisions.

C   ☐   Attaining power is all that matters.

---

1. What is the woman doing?

   A   ☐   agreeing

   B   ☐   disagreeing

   C   ☐   criticising

2. Where are the speakers?

   A   ☐   in a television studio

   B   ☐   in a radio studio

   C   ☐   in a public meeting room

3. What is the speaker accusing the opposition party of doing?

   A   ☐   lying about issues

   B   ☐   ignoring issues

   C   ☐   concealing issues

4. What is the man's attitude towards 'literature'?

   A   ☐   It's not really worth the effort.

   B   ☐   It's inappropriate for his purpose.

   C   ☐   It helps to pass the time.

5. What is the relationship between these speakers?

   A   ☐   bookseller and customer

   B   ☐   librarian and borrower

   C   ☐   two friends who like literature

6. How did the speaker feel when she discovered the narrator was a girl?

A ☐ pleasantly surprised

B ☐ shocked

C ☐ disappointed

7. How can Jenny's behaviour best be described?

A ☐ It was typical.

B ☐ It was unexpected.

C ☐ It was predictable.

8. What is the speaker claiming about lawyers?

A ☐ They are less emotional than other people.

B ☐ They are equally susceptible to emotion as others.

C ☐ Their stressful job makes them emotional.

9. What happened to the players?

A ☐ They were criticised for shouting at the referee.

B ☐ They were punished for pushing the referee.

C ☐ They were reported by the referee.

10. Who is the woman?

A ☐ a friend

B ☐ a therapist

C ☐ a policewoman

Section 2

You will hear a recording about ways of attracting young people to political elections. Listen to the whole recording once. Then you will hear the recording again with pauses for you to write down what you hear. Make sure you spell the words correctly.

11.

Test Tip

Try to resist writing anything during the first reading. Instead concentrate on understanding the overall meaning.

Section 3

You will hear a recorded announcement about a bookstore promotion. First, read the unfinished sentences below, then listen and complete the sentences with information from the announcement.

> **Example:** Customers may not find what they want because of _the new layout_ .

12 The current promotion is to ....

13 Writers from the same family are ....

14 Zola and Proust are examples of ....

15 Only Roth and DeLillo are ....

16 The only title mentioned is ....

You will hear someone arranging to do a counselling course in 'anger management'. First, read the notes below, then listen and complete the notes with information from the conversation.

> **Example:** Name of the programme: _Short Term Counselling_

17 Techniques used: ....

18 The three C's of anger management: ....

19 The negative element of anger: ....

20 Frequency of intensive courses: ....

21 Total number of hours in monthly courses: ....

Section 4

Read each text and put a cross (X) by the missing word or phrase, as in the example.

Example:

If you want a quality steam cleaner for cleaning numerous surfaces in the home, this one gives a high standard of hygiene and kills dust mites and other allergens. It can be used in kitchens and bathrooms, and is also .... for cleaning your upholstery and mattresses.

A   ☒   suitable
B   ☐   proper
C   ☐   prepared

22.

VOTE FOR US

and you vote

TO SAVE THE ENVIRONMENT.
We are the only party
to place the environment at
THE TOP OF ....

A   ☐   local politics
B   ☐   the political agenda
C   ☐   our suggestions

23.

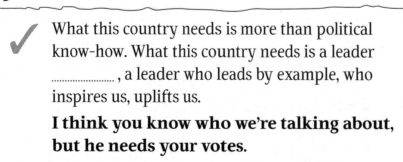

What this country needs is more than political know-how. What this country needs is a leader .... , a leader who leads by example, who inspires us, uplifts us.

I think you know who we're talking about, but he needs your votes.

A   ☐   in a variety of situations
B   ☐   in lots of different countries
C   ☐   in the true sense of the word

24.

> If you want a fantastic read from a really great writer, why not come in and browse though our special offer, classic novels section. .... find something you'll like and you'll like the price too.

A	☐	I hope you'll
B	☐	You're bound to
C	☐	I wonder if you'll

25.

> " *I would like to apologise to all my fans for my behaviour towards the press yesterday afternoon. I was put in a difficult position and was asked some provocative questions, but there is no excuse for .... I hope you will all give me another chance.*

A	☐	my outburst
B	☐	my interest
C	☐	my disappointment

26.

> *Did you feel like screaming at someone today?*
> *Things getting on top of you at work?*
> *Boss making your life a misery?*
> *.................., try our range of relaxing herbal teas and feel the tension of a hard day disappear.*

A	☐	When you get to work
B	☐	When you get up
C	☐	When you get home

Test Tip

It can often help if you imagine where you would see these texts in everyday life. For example, does it come from a magazine, a website, a label?

Section 5

Read the passage and complete the sentences below. Put a cross (X) in the box next to the correct answer, as in the example.

Why aren't youngsters interested in politics?

We're always hearing about apathetic British youth who have no interest in politics or politicians, nor are ever likely to. Is this apparent apathy the result of disillusionment with the political system or simply because life has generally been pretty good to the young in recent years? Supposedly, the "political apathy" referred to has developed because young people, up until the economic crisis and recent parliamentary scandals, have not really had much to worry about in life. So why bother getting involved?

Ironically, this is quite a good thing: no scandal, no economic crisis, no threat to lifestyle, usually equates with high levels of apathy. It's when there are fundamental issues that directly affect individual lives that people make their voices heard and put their voting boots on.

Many young people have always believed that politicians are inherently corrupt and this belief has been compounded by recent political corruption scandals in this country. The reasoning goes that because of a general mistrust of politicians, young people vote with their feet; in other words they don't vote at all. But this view simply doesn't stack up against the facts. Throughout history, whenever there is a national crisis, such as a war with another country, or the miners' strikes of the seventies, or the exposure of some kind of institutional corruption, then that is precisely the time when apathy takes a back seat and people come out to make their feelings known. It's not in human nature for people to get angry about something and then decide not to act on it in order to let the status quo continue.

Politicians who have spent their entire lives actively involved in politics want everyone to be just like them. There are plenty of people in the world to whom politics is just a bore and who want to get on with their real lives. Being young is a time where you can be relatively free of the stress and strain of adult life. Surely, if youngsters prefer to have a good time rather than becoming interested in politics, why shouldn't they? But when there is an issue they care about, then people will become more involved; and later, when they are no longer young and have concerns about job security and taxation, political apathy will disappear. It's clearly not a big problem.

Example: What is the accepted idea about today's youth and politics?

A ☒ Their lack of interest in politics will last.

B ☐ They have a temporary dislike of politics.

C ☐ They like complaining about politicians.

27. What is the suggested reason for youngsters' political apathy?

A ☐ They have insufficient information.

B ☐ They are satisfied with their lives.

C ☐ They generally agree with the politicians.

28. When does the writer think people are more likely to vote?

A ☐ When the economy is going well.

B ☐ When people tell them to do so.

C ☐ When they have specific concerns.

29. What happens to youngsters during national crises?

A ☐ They become less apathetic.

B ☐ They carry on as normal.

C ☐ They get angry, but do nothing.

30. In the writer's view what should youngsters do?

A ☐ contribute more to politics

B ☐ take responsibility in their lives

C ☐ enjoy their years of youth

31. What is the writer's belief about political apathy?

A ☐ Most people outgrow it.

B ☐ There is too much of it.

C ☐ It is disappearing.

Test Tip

Try not to be put off if you find a particular text rather difficult to understand in parts. Try to form an idea of the general meaning and answer the questions in the normal way – you will often find that the questions can be answered even if you don't understand everything in the text. Remember, you aren't expected to write a full answer, but simply choose from three possibilities.

Section 6

Read the article below and answer the questions.

What makes us laugh and why do we laugh? Scientists attempting to answer these questions have found that people who are perceived as witty, clever and funny will be more successful in work and relationships.

A sense of humour may be that missing ingredient to transform a romantic attraction into a flourishing long-term relationship. But whereas women say they want someone who makes them laugh, men say they want someone whom they can make laugh. In another recent survey, 91 percent of top executives surveyed considered humour important to career advancement.

What's more, scientists report that a strong sense of humour speeds healing and reduces the risk of suicide, depression and heart disease. It is humanity's ultimate coping mechanism, smoothing the difficulties of modern life.

Laughter societies hold annual conventions dedicated to researching why we laugh. To them, laughter is much more than a neural-path action triggering the involuntary expulsion of air and sound.

Example: In which two areas of life does a sense of humour make a difference?

Work and relationships

---

32. What do many men like women to appreciate?

....

33. What physical illness can be avoided through humour?

....

34. What does laughter help people to do in life?

....

35. What does the last sentence describe?

....

Section 6 Continued

Read the article below and answer the questions.

HOW DO WE CRY? Tears require an emotional response to be activated, which can be caused by pain or loss of love. When emotions affect us, the nervous system stimulates the brain which sends signals to the tear glands. The lacrimal gland produces the tears of emotion. Scientists believe that the body depends on this gland to release excess amounts of chemicals and hormones, returning it to a stable state.

There are many culturally acceptable reasons to cry in society. The first is probably death. Grieving includes crying and it was often believed that if someone did not cry, they would suffer physically because they did not release their pain. Experiences in life and love are other reasons society allows us to cry. Women have been allowed to cry more than men traditionally, but the benefits of crying seem to suggest that men need to cry more.

Example: What does crying depend on?
          (an) emotional response

36. What do tear glands require before they release tears?

....

37. What accumulates in the body when people get emotional?

....

38. What do people avoid through crying when someone dies?

....

39. Why is it more acceptable for women to cry more than men?

....

Test Tip

When answering questions like this, try to give a full answer, but don't include unnecessary information. Your answer doesn't have to be written as a sentence – often a word or phrase is enough. For example, a full sentence answer to Question 34 might be "Laughter helps people to cope with difficulties in life." But all you really need to write is "cope (with difficulties)."

Read the article below and complete the sentences that follow. Write no more than three words from the article in each gap.

Why do women read more fiction than men?

According to surveys conducted in Britain, the United States and Canada, men account for only 20 percent of the fiction market. In other words, a whopping 80 percent of fiction readers are women. Why should this be so? The theory that too much modern fiction is about feelings and relationships and that's what women want to read, is not borne out by recent research within the publishing industry. This shows, somewhat surprisingly, that women comprise a greater percentage of readers than men across all genres. Here are some of the figures. Espionage/thriller (69 percent); General fiction (88 percent); Mystery/Detective novels (86 percent); and even Science Fiction (52 percent). Macho male critics in the literary world suggest that the school curriculum has been feminized by a diet of touchy-feely books rather than by stories of action and adventure by masculine writers like Ernest Hemingway. But there is no indication that men dislike reading per se, only that women tend to read more fiction. When it comes to non-fiction books, the figures are reversed: men out-read women by at least ten percent.

On the other side of the gender coin, a theory frequently put forward is that women like fiction because they have richer and more complex imaginations. Such arguments reproduce the worst kind of gender stereotypes: women as sensitive, emotionally intelligent creatures; men as unfeeling, inconsiderate idiots.

Maybe men don't like reading novels because the life of a novelist offers few rewards to the traditional male ego. It's not about power, glory and money. No man wants to be like a novelist, shut away alone, writing and rewriting. He wants to be like a professional sportsman or a movie actor.

Perhaps we are moving back to the values of the 19th century, when the novel was considered a low-status pastime of ladies of leisure, rather a waste of time and unfit for real men.

Unfortunately, it is impossible for us to speculate on whether men read more fiction during the 1940s and 50s heyday of macho writers like Hemingway or Jack Kerouac, as there was little relevant research at the time. So, it's hard to establish a definitive link between the size of male readership and the status given to fiction in society – at least over the past 100 years. What is clear is that the novel seems to be reverting to its origins as a feminine hobby, and hence is in danger of being given less credit than it deserves.

Example: One theory is that men don't want to read books about *feelings and relationships* .

40. Women tend to read more fiction than men no matter what the ....

41. Some people say the school curriculum does not study enough novels about ....
....

42. One area where women come second to men is in ....

43. Branding women as sensitive and intelligent and men as inconsiderate is an example of
....

44. Perhaps men don't read so much fiction because they think a novelist's life doesn't have many
....

45. We can't tell whether men used to read more fiction because of insufficient ....

46. We can make a comparison between attitudes towards women and fiction nowadays and those
of ....

Section 8

Use information from Section 7 to help you write your answer.

47. **You have read the article about readers of fiction. Write a response to this article with your own views on the subject for a college magazine. Write about 120–150 words. In your article you should:**
    - explain why you think more women than men read fiction
    - explain what kinds of books your female and male friends read
    - give your views on the importance of reading fiction

Write your answer here. Do not write outside the box.

Section 9

Choose one of the topics below and write your answer in 200–250 words.

48. A) Politics

You see the following entry in a local newspaper.

> Following our interview with local MP Jackie Dodds, during which she stated that being a politician these days was one of the most difficult jobs that exist,
>
> *we are running a competition for the best article entitled*
>
> ## 'So what's so hard about being a politician?'
>
> **The winning entry will be published in the newspaper and the writer will receive a special cash prize.**

Write an essay with this title for submission to the newspaper.

Or

48. B) Emotions

Write an article for a website entitled 'Controlling our emotions'.
Include the following:

- dangers of controlling our emotions at all times
- best circumstances to allow our emotions to be expressed
- how society views the expression of emotions in public

Write your answer here. Do not write outside the box.

Test Tip

Think carefully about which topic to choose from the two options. It may not be the one you are more interested in. Quickly go through in your mind which topic offers more possibilities for you to write about. Do a quick mental plan for each one before making up your mind. Then when you decide, you will have a good idea of what your essay will look like.

Section 10 (2 minutes)

In this section you will speak on your own for about a minute and a half. Listen to what your teacher/examiner asks. Your teacher/examiner will ask one of the main questions below and ask the follow-up questions if necessary.

Main prompt 1:
- In what ways do politics affect your life?

Follow-up prompts:
- Do any of your friends avoid talking about politics? Why?
- Do you think modern politics is more about image than policies? Explain.
- How much do you think you can influence or make changes in your community?
- Which past or present world leaders do you admire? Why?

Main prompt 2:
- How much and what kind of reading do you do?

Follow-up prompts:
- What literature do you remember studying at school?
- Which character from literature would you most like to meet? Why?
- In what way do you think young people should be exposed to good literature?
- Does it matter that children only read books like *Harry Potter*?

Main prompt 3:
- In what way would you describe yourself as an emotional person?

Follow-up prompts:
- Can you describe someone you know who you consider to be an extremely emotional type?
- How do you react if a friend starts crying?
- What kind of things can make you angry?
- How do you think men and women have changed in terms of showing emotions?

Main prompt 4:
- How involved are you in your local community?

Follow-up prompts:
- What kind of problems do you see around you in your local community?
- How do you think you or others should get involved in making life better for people who are less well-off?
- Would you describe yourself as an optimist about the future? Explain.
- How far do you think we should concentrate on solving local problems rather than global ones?

Test Tip

Some questions in Section 10 may focus on something you don't have much to say about. You can always talk around the topic: "I find it difficult to talk about what I'm like or whether I'm very emotional or not. I think you'd have to ask my friends or my family about that. I like to think of myself as a calm sort of person."

Section 11 (2 minutes)

In this section you will discuss something with your teacher/examiner.

> **Do humans have a duty to protect animals and other wildlife?**

What do you think?

Your teacher/examiner will use the following arguments to take an opposing view to yours.

For protecting wildlife:	• It is in our own interest to preserve the balance of nature. • Losing animal and plant species makes the world a poorer place. • It's irresponsible to carry on destroying the world. • Humans have no more right to live on the planet than other species.

Against protecting wildlife:	• It doesn't really matter if a few species are lost. • Humans are more important than animals. • Sometimes protecting wildlife is a sentimental luxury. • Humans have always made nature serve their needs.

Test Tip

There are many expressions to learn to use in a discussion to show agreement and disagreement. Make your views clear and use language to preface your views: "In my experience ... , Personally, I think ... , What I mean is ... , In my opinion ... ."

Section 12 (2 minutes)

In this section you will talk for up to 1 minute about these two pictures of food markets which are being considered for a poster to encourage people to buy food grown locally. Tell your teacher/examiner what you can see in the pictures.

Your teacher/examiner will now put this secondary prompt.

Which one would you choose for a poster to encourage people to buy food grown locally? Why?

> **Test Tip**
>
> *The second part is to choose one of the pictures for a purpose. Make sure you give the reasons for your choice, explaining the impact you think the picture you've chosen would have. Add any information which would enhance the choice, for example: "I think there should be ... as well on the poster."*

Section 13 (2 minutes)

In this section you will take part in a role play with your teacher/examiner. Here is a card with the situation and your goal.

TEST TAKER'S CARD

The situation: You are part of a campaign group protesting against the building of a large road near your town. You have been nominated by your group to speak to the local political leader to present your views.

Your goal: Try to persuade the politician to allow you to present your views to the local council.

Your teacher/examiner is a local political leader and has agreed to meet you to discuss the issue of the new road. Below is a sample script that your teacher/examiner may use.

Ready? I'll start.

Right I haven't got much time so tell me what you wanted to see me about.

Don't you think the new road will solve some of the problems with traffic congestion?

Residents living along the existing road suffer from pollution.

How can the traffic problems be solved without this new road?

The road will be good for the economy as drivers won't be delayed in traffic.

We can use the land around the new road for new businesses and homes.

(Agree to allowing the protestor to speak for 5 minutes at the next council meeting.)

That is the end of the test.

Unit Three

The themes for this unit are: history/character/higher education/books and reading

Vocabulary and Grammar

Vocabulary 1: Collocation

Match each word on the left with one from the right and then complete the sentences that follow, as in the example.

~~higher~~	manner
terrific	grade
eye	survey
career	class
threatening	accuracy
historical	contact
final	performance
authoritative	height
working	~~education~~
nationwide	path
average	behaviour

Example: After completing secondary school, it was always assumed I would proceed to ..higher.. ..education.. at a top university.

1 A .... found that more young people are applying to attend university than ever before.

2 Although he had studied hard throughout the year, his .... was a disappointment to both him and his tutors.

3 Although he is only of .... , he seems to grow in stature every time he walks on to the sports field.

4 Although very young to be such a high position, it was the king's .... that gained his subjects' respect.

5 By the time he was seventeen he had already planned out his .... all the way through to retirement.

6 It was his .... towards his colleagues which finally got him suspended from the university.

7 Thanks to a .... by the entire team, they won the game.

8 The gap between rich and poor had never been greater, with conditions in the London slums making life impossible for the ....

9 The golden rule for interviews is to always maintain .... with the person interviewing you.

10 The most astounding thing about her novels is their .... , so you learn a lot about the period whilst enjoying an exciting story.

Vocabulary 2: Phrasal verbs

Complete each sentence with the correct form of a phrasal verb, as in the example. Each phrasal verb has two different meanings and so will be used twice.

| catch up | deal with | depend on | get on | look around |
| look at | put in | ~~run out~~ | send out | take down | think of |

Example: When the fire started, the occupants .**ran out**. of the house.
He stayed in Paris until he .**ran out**. of money.

1 He .... me with suspicion.

2 Every time he heard that music, he .... his childhood in the countryside.

3 Thank you for being patient. We'll .... the results to everyone this week.

4 Although they left several hours later, they managed to .... with the other group.

5 As the information was released, the man .... the details in his notebook.

6 He was a ruthless leader who .... his opponents cruelly.

7 He heard a sound behind him and .... to see who it was.

8 He .... for the post of senior lecturer.

9 All great leaders .... the quality of their advisers.

10 If you want to do well, you'll just have to .... with your work.

11 The new higher education policy .... the wrong message to students.

12 They had to .... the building because they had no planning permission.

13 Long before you leave school, it pays to .... for some courses that you like.

14 It's a lovely gift and it's so good of you to .... me.

15 I hope he does well in his exams; he has certainly .... the work.

16 Getting into that university .... your exam results.

17 I'm afraid it's your problem, so you'll have to .... it.

18 We'll have to .... ways in which we can raise the money.

19 He couldn't join his friends at the party because he had to .... with some work.

20 It is an open secret that the two men didn't .... with each other.

Grammar 1: Relative clauses

Complete the sentences in one of the following ways:

A add a comma plus a relative clause, 'who', 'which' or 'where'.

B add 'that' or 'who' (without a comma) where possible.

C add nothing where possible.

Examples: The books, **which** should be helpful for you, are arriving later.
Here are the books **that** will help you with your course.
These are the books ------ you need for your course.

1 He was the kind of character .... they needed.

2 The girl .... lived very near him, got a first class honours at university.

3 He found his easy temperament allowed him to get on with almost everybody .... made him very popular.

4 It was a decision .... was to change the course of history.

5 He was introduced to his new head of department .... shook his hand warmly.

6 The girl .... he married was to become an influential figure throughout the country.

7 This is the man .... can help you.

8 They first met in the village of Hampton .... they married four years later.

9 He told me something .... I'll never forget.

10 It was the same company .... had rejected him six years before.

Grammar 2: Passive sentences

Change each sentence into the passive form, using the verb in brackets, as in the example.

Example: People think this development may be the first of many.
(see)

This development may be seen as the first of many . .

1 People thought that it was the best of its kind.
(consider)

....

2 People have found that the project lacks financial support.
(find)

....

3 The number of university applications will probably reach an all-time high this year.
(believe)

....

....

4 Her classmates are suggesting that the girl knew the man.
(put forward)

....

5 People think they had known each other for some years.
(suggest)

....

6 They claimed nothing illegal had taken place.
(deny)

....

7 Many think they already knew each other.
(assume)

....

8 They thought he would arrive the next day.
(expect)

....

9 The writing of the new education programme took three years.
(develop)

....

10 We have to make these cuts in order to offset shortfalls in higher education finance.
(need)

....

Grammar 3: Modals

Rewrite these sentences using an appropriate modal phrase, as in the example. There may be more than one possible answer. Use: *should/could/may/might/would/must*.

Example: I'm absolutely certain he has arrived by now.

He _must have arrived by now_ .

1 It's possible that his strength of character got him through.
His ....

2 I'm not sure if I can attend the lecture tomorrow.
I ....

3 I'm sure he wasn't Prime Minister during the Second World War; I'm certain it was later.
He ....

....

4 I suppose his stubbornness is just part of his character.
His ....

5 The president refused to end sanctions against the country.
The ....

6 I don't think that he got the application form to the college on time.
He ....

7 It's possible that the course did not cover the content of the exam.
The course ....

8 It wasn't a good idea for him to make such comments at the time.
He ....

9 I'm sure he had the strength of character to stand up to this man and refuse.
He ....

10 Did you not think of telling them earlier?

.... ?

Language skills

◉ Listening 1: Listening for key information

Listen to the following recording about character and pick out three key ideas.

1 Business excellence requires: ....

2 Character can be: ....

3 The character of business leaders needs to be: ....

⊙ Listening 2: Listening for detail

Listen to the same recording again and answer the following questions.

1 What is excellence sometimes confused with? ....

2 What aspects of leadership should be considered? ....

3 How does the speaker describe a strong character? ....

4 How does the speaker describe a weak character? ....

5 Which two examples are given to describe good and bad strong characters? ....
....

6 What·is an important element that a leader should have? ....

Reading and listening: Sentence and note completion

Read the following script from a talk about reading groups. Candidates are expected to listen to such texts and complete notes using words from the text. Predict what the candidate could be asked by writing three sentences with blanks to be completed with information from the text.

Example: Reading groups were started by females in *factories* .

> **Text**
>
> Did you know that the first recorded reading groups were among women working in factories in the nineteenth century? Reading is normally a solitary activity, but how often do you read a book and talk to someone else about it? Reading groups allow you to share your enjoyment of books.
>
> And now, according to research undertaken a few years ago, there are tens of thousands of groups meeting regularly in the UK reading everything from literary classics to technical manuals!

Compare your sentences with gaps with those given below.

1 The conventional view is that reading is a .... thing to do.

2 The popularity of reading groups is demonstrated by the .... in existence in the UK.

3 A surprising choice of some reading groups is ....

Now complete the blanks for sentences 1–3.

⊙ Read sentences 4–7 below, then listen to the text to complete the gaps.

4 The different rules of reading groups demonstrate that none are ....

5 Readers need to be aware that a particular book may have a .... which is inappropriate.

6 Libraries have a service which provides .... of chosen books.

7 The book list for reading groups is updated with ....

Writing: Paragraph organisation

Rewrite the following sentences in the correct order to make one paragraph. The first one is given as an example.

1 He was reluctant to test on humans for fear it might not work.

2 Soon Louis and his team were working around the clock to save people who had rabies.

3 The treatment was a success and news soon spread.

4 There is no doubt that, more than any other person, Louis Pasteur helped to increase the life expectancy of man in modern times.

5 Although the famous scientist treated thousands of cases, he took a personal interest in every individual patient.

6 However, the parents of a young boy who had been bitten by a rabid dog insisted he try his new technique.

7 ~~Louis Pasteur created a cure for rabies – a very common disease in the 19th century.~~

8 Louis Pasteur worked tirelessly to deliver real benefits for the treatment of infectious diseases.

9 On one of the rare occasions when he failed and a ten-year-old girl died, the great scientist was desperately upset.

10 He found that by giving animals a weakened form of the illness they were able to develop immunity.

Louis Pasteur created a cure for rabies – a very common disease in the 19th century.

Practice Test Three

Section 1

You will have 10 seconds to read each question and the corresponding options. Then listen to the recording. After the recording you will have 10 seconds to choose the correct option. Put a cross (X) in the box next to the correct answer, as in the example.

> **Example:** What is this man describing?
>
> A ☐ the site of a battle
> B ☐ a ship-building site
> C ☒ the site of a castle

1. What is the conclusion of these speakers about history?
   A ☐ It doesn't change our behaviour.
   B ☐ It doesn't teach us anything.
   C ☐ It doesn't follow a pattern.

2. What is the teacher doing?
   A ☐ insisting
   B ☐ advising
   C ☐ ordering

3. What does the man want to do with the book?
   A ☐ read it
   B ☐ sell it
   C ☐ keep it

4. This man is advising his friend about a meeting. What kind of meeting?
   A ☐ with business clients
   B ☐ a job interview
   C ☐ a planning meeting

5. What kind of sport is the speaker describing?
   A ☐ a game between two teams
   B ☐ a tournament between several teams
   C ☐ a race between several teams

6. What is the relationship between the speakers?

A ☐ a furniture salesman and a customer

B ☐ a couple discussing furniture at home

C ☐ a houseowner and a man delivering furniture

7. What does the speaker imply about going to university?

A ☐ It can reward you if you work hard.

B ☐ It can guarantee you a good job.

C ☐ It can help you make useful contacts.

8. What is the man's advice?

A ☐ Don't worry about failing.

B ☐ Rise to the challenge.

C ☐ Think about how important it is.

9. What is the caller's attitude towards the student loan office?

A ☐ He appreciates that they are doing their best.

B ☐ He thinks they don't appreciate the difficulties.

C ☐ He appreciates the woman's concern.

10. Why does the speaker like the actor's portrayal of the vampire?

A ☐ He lets us see the human side.

B ☐ He builds the character.

C ☐ He keeps it straightforward.

Section 2

 You will hear a recording about characterisation in novels. Listen to the whole recording once. Then you will hear the recording again with pauses for you to write down what you hear. Make sure you spell the words correctly.

11.

Section 3

You will hear a university tutor addressing a group of students about ways to improve the delivery of their presentations. First, read the notes below, then listen and complete the notes with information from the talk.

> **Example:** Many students giving a presentation believe they simply have to *recite/read what they know* .

12 The level of attention from listeners depends on the presenter's ....

13 Watching a video of your presentation not only helps you identify what needs to improve, but also ....

14 Good presentations should resemble ....

15 No matter how well you do it, reading from notes makes it difficult to ....

16 It could be said that the most important part of your presentation is ....

You will hear two radio presenters discussing the effect of historical inaccuracy in film. First, read the notes below, then listen and complete the notes with information from the discussion.

The discussion is about the importance of (**Example:**) *historical accuracy* in film. The woman suggests that because some film makers distort the facts, they are behaving 17 .... On the other hand, the man thinks that changing some historical detail sometimes results in 18 .... The woman feels that after seeing a historical film some people may want to 19 .... But she also thinks that films like U-571 change the facts so much they make the film 20 .... Unfortunately, film makers can only be challenged on film content if they state that the film is 21 ....

> **Test Tip**
> *Use the pause before the recording starts to read the beginnings of the notes carefully so that you know exactly what you are listening for. In note-completion exercises, although you can't predict the answers, it's sometimes possible to predict the topic or the kind of information you will hear.*

Section 4

Read each text and put a cross (X) by the missing word or phrase, as in the example.

Example:

> Autobiographies tend to be commercial exercises. Very few autobiographies qualify as great literature, ... those written by great writers.

A   [X]   even

B   ☐   especially

C   ☐   rather than

22.

> He writes lucidly and informatively of the shaping of post–war Britain through the creation of a solid background .... flashes of illuminating detail.

A   ☐   included in

B   ☐   highlighted by

C   ☐   exemplified by

23.

> We are one of the UK's leading universities, with an acknowledged reputation for excellence. We offer high standards of education to everyone with the ability to benefit, ... their economic circumstances. Our courses are challenging and rigorous, guided and inspired by our first-class academic staff.

A   ☐   regardless of

B   ☐   depending on

C   ☐   subject to

24.

> *I chose history because, quite frankly, I didn't know .... But I'm pleased to say it was one of the best decisions I ever made in my life.*

A   ☐   much about it

B   ☐   what it involved

C   ☐   how it was taught

25.

Tonight's debating society event is entitled:

'Knowledge for .... or knowledge for practical application'.

What do students want to get from their university course?

Come along and join in.

A ☐ its own sake

B ☐ useful purposes

C ☐ specific subjects

26.

Kids often learn more from their sports coaches about character than about athletic performance. Here are some tools to help you .... the character-building potential of your sports programme.

A ☐ work at

B ☐ train for

C ☐ benefit from

Section 5

Read the passage and answer the questions below. Put a cross (X) in the box next to the correct answer, as in the example.

According to some people, a university degree is a waste of time and money, leaving graduates not only in serious debt, but also worse off in terms of job prospects and pay expectations than school-leavers. Are they right? Or is university still a worthwhile experience? We asked for your views. Here's what you said.

A

I graduated with a law degree eight years ago and was told it was a degree that was widely recognised by employers and useful in getting a well-paid graduate job. Nothing could have been further from the truth. University is a con and only suits the middle classes.

B

I'm just starting university and I think the whole experience is going to be great. I'll be studying Psychology and I hope to get a career as a chartered psychologist. The fact that I'll be in debt after my four years there doesn't bother me too much, although it would be nice to avoid it. But I don't really mind how much I get paid after I graduate.

C

I'm a university lecturer. I don't think university is a waste of time, but I feel that, although graduates get a lot of advice about their courses, it should include advice about where their degree will take them and their likely salary prospects. Many of my undergraduate students either believe they will earn high salaries within six months of leaving university, or are scared stiff that they won't find a job and have a mountain of debt to pay off. The truth is it's probably somewhere in between.

D

My worry about universities is that there is too much emphasis on getting 'bums on seats' and that often means accepting people who really aren't up to it, either academically or personality-wise. Students who leave with 3rd class degrees after turning up to the minimum of lectures, are wasting their time. They can't get a decent job and they are burdened with huge debts.

E

Thirteen years ago I left school at sixteen without any qualifications. Some friends stayed on and went to university. Maybe it was right for them. But I got a job and after a lot of hard work I'm earning a good salary and enjoy my job. My graduate friends are either struggling in low-paid, unfulfilling jobs or have no work at all. Maybe I missed out on university life, but no piece of paper can equate to the practical experience I have had.

Example: What does A believe about what he was told?

A ☒ It was misleading.

B ☐ It is only partly true.

C ☐ It was helpful advice.

---

27. What is most important to B apart from his qualification?

A ☐ having good salary prospects

B ☐ avoiding too much debt

C ☐ experiencing university life

28. What does C think about advice given to students?

A ☐ It can be a waste of time.

B ☐ It omits important issues.

C ☐ There isn't enough of it.

29. What does C think about the beliefs of his students?

A ☐ They are too extreme.

B ☐ They are realistic.

C ☐ They are over-optimistic.

30. In what way does D worry about university policy?

A ☐ They have lowered their expectations.

B ☐ They have lowered their teaching standards.

C ☐ They have lowered their entry criteria.

31. What is E's view of his graduate friends?

A ☐ They made the wrong choice.

B ☐ They have been disappointed.

C ☐ They didn't work hard enough.

Test Tip

Often, you will find that each question refers to a paragraph or a block of text, so you have an idea where to look for the answers. In this particular section, there is an introductory paragraph followed by paragraphs A to E. Each question corresponds to a paragraph. It won't always be this straightforward, but more often than not you will be able to judge where to look for the answer to each question. Learn to look for answers to questions in a logical way like this.

Section 6

Read the article below and answer the questions.

In the 19th century, the Industrial Revolution transformed life in Britain. Whereas before, most people lived and worked on farmland, many now moved to towns to work in industry. Whilst the place of middle-class women was at home, the life of working-class women was an endless round of hard work and drudgery. As soon as they were old enough, often well before their tenth birthday, they worked in factories until they married and had children of their own. The very high mortality rate meant that families were much larger than today. People just assumed that not all their children would survive, partly because of disease but also because of fatal accidents at work.

The father was the head of the family. His wife and children respected him and obeyed him and, until 1882, all a woman's property, even the money she earned, belonged to her husband. Divorce was made legal in 1857 but it was very rare in the 19th century.

Example: What kind of work had people done before the Industrial Revolution?
        farm work

---

32. Apart from children, what determined whether or not a woman stayed at home?

....

33. What ended girls' factory work?

....

34. Who was the main person in the family?

....

35. Which law made little difference in practice?

....

Test Tip

It is to be expected that some questions might seem easier than others. Check through the questions in this section and identify the ones you think you may be able to answer first. The texts are quite short, so this should be fairly straightforward. This provides a good basis for you to move on to the more difficult ones.

Section 6 continued

Read the article below and answer the questions.

In an attempt to get ahead of their rivals in a job market that is becoming ever more competitive, about 25,000 UK students a year are choosing to stay on after completing their first degrees, to take on a postgraduate degree. They believe that it will make them more employable, and with good reason.

As well as offering students the chance to train in a new profession, postgraduate study can also offer students the opportunity to gain a greater degree of specialisation in their existing career path.

But whilst an extra qualification on your CV can be useful, it is not all that is needed to catch the eye of an employer.

Most employers of graduates do not distinguish between a postgraduate and good undergraduate qualifications; what they are also looking for is potential and the ability to learn on the job. But the icing on the cake is relevant work experience, which many regard as just as important as a qualification.

Example: What is happening to the graduate job market?

It is becoming more competitive .

36. What is the writer's view of the students' belief in the first paragraph?

....

37. What does postgraduate study offer students who don't want to change their subject?

....

38. For employers, what is the difference between postgraduates and graduates?

....

39. What is equally as good as a qualification in the eyes of employers?

....

Read the article below and complete the questions that follow. Write no more than three words from the article in each gap.

What exactly is
CHARACTER BUILDING?

Can we develop strength of character in our children or is it just a natural thing? Character building can be developed if we give our children the right experiences in the right environment through the right education. Character education should include everyone. It isn't complicated and it's based on some basic values that are not political, religious, or culturally biased. Children find it easy to understand these values and their logic right from the start. Here's what we should be helping our children with every day.

Be honest with yourself and towards others. Avoid deceit, cheating or stealing. Do what you say you'll do and build up a reputation amongst others of being reliable and consistent. This will be respected more than anything else about you. Do the right thing, even if it's easier not to. Be loyal to friends and family.

Treat those around you with the respect you would expect from them. Learn to tolerate differences between yourself and others and make those differences into a positive thing. Be civil and respectful to those around you. Consider the feelings of others and avoid threatening behaviour. If someone gets angry with you, deal with it as peacefully and constructively as you are able and try to think what has made the person angry in the first place.

Develop a sense of responsibility, first of all to yourself and your values, then to others. Do what you are supposed to do, keep trying and always do your best. Develop self-discipline and think before you act. Consider the consequences of your actions and be accountable for your choices.

Be fair and avoid becoming greedy. Take turns and share, be open-minded and, most importantly, listen to others. Don't take advantage of other people's weaknesses.

Don't play the blame game. It's sometimes nobody's fault. Be kind, show compassion and show you care for others. Be grateful when you need to be, forgive others willingly. Show a willingness to help other people who need to be helped.

Become a good citizen, no matter what your circumstances. Help make your community better every day. Cooperate with others and don't assume things will get done without you. Stay informed and be a good neighbour. Abide by the laws and the rules, even if you think some are unreasonable. There are other ways of changing them. Respect authority. Protect the environment.

> **Example:** Providing children with appropriate experiences and education helps *develop/build* *(their) character.*

40. The values of character education are ....

41. The things that will earn other people's respect are ....

42. If someone gets angry with you, avoid ....

43. Don't take any action without ....

44. If other people are not as strong as you, ...

45. Accept that a failure is sometimes the fault of ....

46. By contributing to your community you can ....

> **Test Tip**
> In this section, as in all note-completion tasks, make sure that what you write is a grammatically correct 'fit' with the surrounding notes (even though notes won't necessarily be complete sentences). For example, in Questions 42 and 43, a gerund (-ing form) is required in each, not an infinitive.

Section 8

Use information from Section 7 to help you write your answer.

47. **You have read the article about character building for children. Write a response to this article with your own views on the subject for a college magazine. Write about 120–150 words. In your article you should:**
    - give some examples of when you need to show strong character
    - describe the ways in which your own education helped develop your character
    - comment on your own strengths and weaknesses of character

Write your answer here. Do not write outside the box.

Section 9

Choose one of the topics below and write your answer in 200–250 words.

48. A) History
You see the following editorial entry in a magazine.

> *During a recent visit to a secondary school, I was appalled at the lack of basic historical knowledge shown by many of the pupils. I would like to start a campaign to get kids more interested in history in order to convince them of its importance to our own lives. We'll start with a writing competition entitled 'What's so important about history?'*

Write an essay with this title for submission to the magazine.

Or

48. B) Higher education
Write an article for a website entitled 'Is higher education worth it?'
Include the following:

- the advantages and disadvantages of continuing your academic education after leaving school
- why some people choose to work even though they have qualified for university entry
- describe your own experience or plans in the field of higher education

Write your answer here. Do not write outside the box.

Section 10 (2 minutes)

In this section you will speak on your own for about a minute and a half. Listen to what your teacher/examiner asks. Your teacher/examiner will ask one of the main questions below and ask the follow-up questions if necessary.

Main prompt 1:
- What college or university courses have you done or would you like to do and how do you get on to such courses?

Follow-up prompts:
- If you could get on to any university course anywhere, where would you choose and why?
- What are the challenges in your country to studying at college/university?
- How do families have to help students to study at college or university?
- Is it easy to get a job in your country if you have a university degree?

Main prompt 2:
- How would different family members describe your character?

Follow-up prompts:
- In what way are you either introverted or extroverted?
- In what way do you think different personalities learn a language better?
- In what ways have you ever behaved out of character?
- How much do you think your character is defined by genes or by upbringing?

Main prompt 3:
- What aspects of your family's history have been passed on to you and would you pass on to your children?

Follow-up prompts:
- What traditions do your family keep going?
- How important do you think it is to study your country's history?
- What do you remember about your history lessons at school?
- Who would be your favourite person from history to learn more about?

Main prompt 4:
- Which book would you recommend that your friends read and why?

Follow-up prompts:
- What kind of books do you like to read?
- How much and what kind of reading do you do in English?
- It's said that reading is the best way to improve your English. How far do you think this is true for you?
- Which is the most memorable book from your childhood? Why?

Section 11 (2 minutes)

In this section you will discuss something with your teacher/examiner.

> Are cities a major cause of environmental problems?

What do you think?

Your teacher/examiner will use the following arguments to take an opposing view to yours.

For cities causing environmental problems:	<ul><li>Large urban areas create a lot of waste.</li><li>Cities tend to be industrial, which creates a lot of pollution.</li><li>People who live in cities have lost touch with nature so care less about it.</li><li>The spread of cities takes up a lot of space which used to be countryside.</li></ul>

Against cities causing environmental problems:	<ul><li>There are more important environmental problems we should be concentrating on, like the destruction of rainforests.</li><li>It's more important to make sure everyone lives more sustainably, not only those in cities.</li><li>Having a lot of people in one area means that there is more use of shared transport.</li><li>People have to live somewhere – the problem is over-population, not cities.</li></ul>

> **Test Tip**
>
> *In this section, the examiner may disagree with you or challenge your opinions. Respond to these challenges by either agreeing or disagreeing, making your opinion clear. Your views may be prefaced with several expressions such as "You may be right, but … , That may be true, but I still think … , But what about … ? I think you should consider … ."*

Section 12 (2 minutes)

In this section you will talk for up to 1 minute about these two pictures about maths teaching. These pictures are being considered for a book on maths teaching. Tell your teacher/examiner what you can see in the pictures.

Your teacher/examiner will now ask this follow-up question.

Which picture would you choose for a book on maths teaching? Why?

> **Test Tip**
>
> *In this section you will be asked to choose which picture is suitable for a particular purpose. Make sure you understand the purpose and include this when giving your opinion. For example, "This picture matches the title of the book better as it looks as though the contents would be fun and interesting."*

Section 13 (2 minutes)

In this section you will take part in a role play with your teacher/examiner. Here is a card with the situation and your goal.

TEST TAKER'S CARD

The situation: You are a student and the college library has cancelled your library card, preventing you from borrowing books. You have always returned books on time. You visit the library to sort out the problem.

Your goal: Persuade the librarian there's been some mistake.

You are a student. Your teacher/examiner is the college librarian. Below is a sample script that your teacher/examiner may use.

Ready? You start.

Let me just check. Yes I'm afraid you can't borrow books until next semester.

The library rules are really clear. You've got 20 penalty points for late return of books.

Our records show the late returns quite clearly.

It may be possible there's a mix-up.

How do you spell your family name? And your initials?

Which faculty are you in?

There's another (say test taker's name) in a different faculty.

It looks as though there's been a mix-up.

Test Tip

The role play may ask you to achieve a goal which requires you to be politely insistent. For example, "Could you please check again as I'm sure there's been some mistake." "I'm sorry, but I'm absolutely sure I've returned all my books on time."

That is the end of the test.

Unit Four

Vocabulary and Grammar

Vocabulary 1: Collocations

Match each word on the left with one from the right and then complete the sentences that follow, as in the example. Add any necessary articles.

overwhelming	opportunity
performance-related	evil
~~tired~~	look
necessary	scale
radically	remunerated
potentially	evidence
ideal	role
lavishly	opposed
global	pay
forbidding	cataclysmic
broader	~~thinking~~

Example: The research into alternative medicine is based on ‥the tired thinking‥ of the pharmaceutical industry.

1 He decided it was .... to restructure the organisation.

2 The latest management style embraces flatter structures and .... for each senior manager.

3 The desolate places in the world have .... , but are havens for wildlife.

4 Conservationists are .... to the culling of badgers to prevent tuberculosis in cattle.

5 Some say that earthquakes, tsunamis and other such natural events are more .... than any man-made effect on the climate.

6 Governments are ignoring .... which shows the world's fish stocks are declining at an unsustainable pace.

7 At one end of the scale are .... leaders of big business and at the other, office and factory workers hardly able to subsist.

8 The new manager has introduced a new system of .... designed to increase productivity.

9 Although it seems cruel, a controlled cull in which animals are selectively killed is sometimes regarded as a ....

10 The accelerating loss of natural habitats is a disaster on a ....

Vocabulary 2: Particles

Use the following words to complete the sentences, as in the example. Add the correct particle to each verb. (Note that one word requires two particles.) Change the verb to be grammatically correct.

wipe   come   be adept   boil   ~~border~~   cross   improve   look   take   pick   draw

Example: His unique management style was considered by his detractors as <u>bordering on</u> the insane.

1 It's of great concern that certain species are facing being .... in our lifetime.

2 As the economy .... speed, we would expect a return to investment in research and development.

3 These creatures .... camouflaging themselves, preventing attacks from predators.

4 The challenges of leadership require those in this role to .... all the resources available to them.

5 The management felt there was no way they could .... levels of productivity as all traditional methods had been tried.

6 It was on a remote Pacific island that the naturalist .... what was to be the last of these species.

7 Some city slums have .... into what are self-sustaining communities.

8 It is no easy task to .... and win the argument against the global petrochemical companies.

9 We .... ways of using urban spaces to grow vegetables and now offer grants to residents for this use.

10 With all the talk about how to improve education, school success .... the quality of the head teacher.

Vocabulary 3: Words with similar meanings

Choose the correct word to complete each of the following sentences, as in the example.

Example: Every piece of research <u>points</u> to the link between pay and productivity.
  A directs   **B** guides   **(C)** points

1 Environmentalists need to keep in .... that politicians have short-term aims.
  A mind   **B** focus   **C** heart

2 The term 'wilderness' is .... defined and covers a number of interpretations.
  A loosely   **B** faintly   **C** thinly

3 Effective leadership plays a significant role in the .... of shareholder rewards.
  A bidding   **B** requirement   **C** delivery

4 The conclusion that all technology improves living standards is .... to interpretation.
  A subject   **B** liable   **C** likely

5 To argue that cities are like living organisms is far too ....
  A immature   **B** credulous   **C** simplistic

6 The disappearance of many British birds is blamed on the _____ use of pesticides in farming.

    A expanded   **B** extensive   **C** extended

7 The city's leaders _____ the idea of cycling by providing bikes which could be hired throughout the city.

    A fostered   **B** assembled   **C** bred

8 More research needs to be _____ to establish how to motivate staff to perform to their maximum capacity.

    A conducted   **B** accomplished   **C** discharged

9 There is little understanding of why porpoises _____ into shallow waters and beach themselves.

    A direct   **B** bear   **C** head

10 There have to be financial _____ to encourage fishermen to reduce their catches to sustainable levels.

    A stimulants   **B** incentives   **C** magnetism

Grammar 1: Passive sentences

Rewrite each of the following using a passive form, as in the example.

Example: Someone needs to conduct the research independently.

    The research needs to be conducted independently .

1 You must see it to believe it.

    ....

2 They have offered the post to someone in marine conservation.

    ....

3 We are outsourcing the routine jobs.

    ....

4 We can no longer attract the most talented into leadership roles.

    ....

5 Our entrepreneurs need a clear strategic vision.

    ....

6 Someone is contacting the CEO first thing tomorrow.

    ....

7 It was expected that the pollution would cause no lasting damage.

    ....

8 The government should have done more to protect the wildlife.

    ....

9 You will be able to witness the migration of wildebeest during August.

    ....

10 They had requested the head teacher's resignation to give them time to recruit her replacement.

    ....

Grammar 2: Sentence patterns

Circle the constructions which can complete the sentences, as in the example. There may be more than one correct answer.

Example: Many of us tend ....

    A to feel overwhelmed by the scale of some environmental problems.

    B not to get involved with those aspects of the environment we can't control.

    C that the main problems of the environment need government action.

1   In-house training is now considered ....

    A a better option for older employees.

    B as if better value for money.

    C to be preferable to conferences.

2   Any new technology is bound to ....

    A being expensive initially.

    B have a negative impact.

    C the result of a long lead in.

3   Effective leaders appear ....

    A sharing the same basic skill set.

    B that inspiring staff is fundamental.

    C to maintain a high visibility.

4   Modern life in cities is unlikely ....

    A to be the choice of the more elderly.

    B be so good for the less well-off.

    C improving without affordable transport.

5   I suppose ....

    A scientific evidence is required.

    B that some scientists will disagree.

    C as if the idea has been tested.

Language skills

◉ Listening and writing: Dictation

You will hear a recording about garden cities. Listen to the whole recording once. Then you will hear the recording again with pauses for you to write down what you hear. Make sure you spell the words correctly.

Speaking: Describing pictures

Look at the following pictures and discuss the questions below.

1 What is happening in the pictures?

2 Which picture best illustrates the idea of bringing the countryside into the city?

3 People living in cities are increasingly cut off from the realities of country life and nature. How far do you see this as a problem?

4 How can children who are brought up in cities be made more aware of nature?

Writing: Complex sentences

Rewrite the following as a single sentence starting with the expression given, as in the example.

Example: Aspiring leaders may succeed in the role. There is a strong health warning for them. They may be ultimately forced to leave it prematurely. There is a high risk. While in the role they will have a limited life outside work. The job will put tremendous strain on health, happiness and close family relationships.

Even if they ...

Possible answer:

Even if they succeed in the role, there is a strong health warning for aspiring leaders, who may ultimately be forced to leave it prematurely as there is a high risk that, while in the role, they will have a limited life outside work and that the job will put tremendous strain on health, happiness, and close family relationships.

1   The new collapsible plastic shipping container is made of fibreglass composite. This means it weighs only three-quarters as much as a standard container. More importantly, it can be folded down to a quarter of its size. This is when it is empty.

Because ...

2   Collapsed containers are bundled together in groups of four. This means ships could be loaded more quickly. This would cut the time spent in ports. This takes up less space on land. It allows depots to operate more efficiently.

If ...

3   Some street art is crossing over towards a more formally recognised form of art in some places. This is a positive trend. This trend has significant cultural and political implications for the city.

The fact that ...

Practice Test Four

Section 1

You will have 10 seconds to read each question and the corresponding options. Then listen to the recording. After the recording you will have 10 seconds to choose the correct option. Put a cross (X) in the box next to the correct answer, as in the example.

Example: How does the speaker feel?

A ☒ sceptical

B ☐ cynical

C ☐ suspicious

---

1. The speakers are expressing

    A ☐ mistrust.

    B ☐ criticism.

    C ☐ dismay.

2. The speaker is talking about

    A ☐ a business broadcast.

    B ☐ a management course.

    C ☐ a leadership textbook.

3. The speaker is recommending

    A ☐ city guidebooks.

    B ☐ travel magazines.

    C ☐ web directories.

4. What are both speakers' attitudes to the person being talked about?

    A ☐ He's unreasonably pessimistic.

    B ☐ His opinions are really reliable.

    C ☐ He holds beliefs in spite of evidence.

5. The man needs to

    A ☐ follow a special diet.

    B ☐ provide more evidence.

    C ☐ watch his weight.

6. The suggestion in the announcement is that
A ☐ hunting for food addresses the problems of local people.
B ☐ killing animals and conserving nature are incompatible.
C ☐ there may be a case for hunting in terms of preserving wildlife.

7. The speaker's view is that financial directors
A ☐ have shown they can take on a broader role.
B ☐ are most useful in harsher financial times.
C ☐ are frightened of a higher profile role.

8. The speaker is implying that any evidence is
A ☐ uncertain.
B ☐ extreme.
C ☐ biased.

9. The speaker assumes that his audience will
A ☐ become aware of the threats facing the natural world.
B ☐ remember that we rely on insects for survival.
C ☐ campaign against the destruction of insects.

10. The speaker's view of squatter cities is that they
A ☐ support poor people.
B ☐ create new cities.
C ☐ develop black markets.

Test Tip
At this level there are only small differences between the choices given. Read the choices and predict what to listen for to make the right choice. For example, in Question 3, what vocabulary would indicate the difference between a guidebook, a magazine or a web directory?

Section 2

You will hear a recording about the meaning of 'wilderness'. Listen to the whole recording once. Then you will hear the recording again with pauses for you to write down what you hear. Make sure you spell the words correctly.

11. ....

....

....

....

....

....

....

....

....

....

....

....

....

Test Tip

Focus on the meaning when you listen first. This will help establish the sentence structure. If you hear a word you don't recognise, don't hesitate. Leave a blank and make a guess at the end.

Section 3

You will hear an interview about volcanoes. First, read the notes below, then listen and complete the notes with information from the interview.

Example: Volcanoes are important as ..*symbols*.. to show the earth is alive.

---

12 Iceland is where the Eurasian and .... tectonic plates meet.

13 If there were no .... , there'd be no magnetic field.

14 The planet .... provides evidence of why volcanoes are vital.

15 The two volcanoes are known as ....

16 The larger volcano has a crater which is .... wide.

You will hear part of a lecture. First, read the notes below, then listen and complete the notes with information from the lecture.

Example: Sand dunes created by: ..*the constant gale*..

---

17 Winter temperatures: ....

18 Location of the civet cats: ....

19 Number of unique life forms: ....

20 Reason behind the name 'dragon's blood': ....

21 Historical evidence of Socotri cows: ....

Test Tip

The answers needed are concrete facts and information and are exact words from the text.
Listen for paraphrases to identify the information, for example in Question 15 "are known as"
paraphrases "so-called".

Section 4

Read each text and put a cross (X) by the missing word or phrase, as in the example.

Example:

There's some temptation to treat the biosphere holistically and the species that compose it as hardly worth distinguishing one from the other. But each is exquisitely adapted to the environment in which it lives, ... to form ecosystems upon which our own lives depend.

- A ☐ living independent lives
- B ☐ displaying great diversity
- C ☒ interlocked with other species

22.

Want to stay up to date with the latest science, health, technology and environment news?

.... to receive free email updates of **SCIENCE FOR TODAY**'s top headlines – delivered to your inbox at no charge. Get the latest science news with our **FREE EMAIL NEWSLETTERS,** updated daily and weekly.

- A ☐ Claim now
- B ☐ Sign up
- C ☐ Join in

23.

TV A biochemist explains that cooking is all about chemistry, and knowing some facts can help chefs understand why recipes go wrong. Because cooking is essentially a ....

- A ☐ series of chemical reactions
- B ☐ parade of scientific steps
- C ☐ lesson following basic recipes

24.

> The Head of Conservation will .... in the delivery of a strategy for protection of the marine environment. This is an ideal opportunity for an experienced, team-oriented individual, with a working background in marine conservation, excellent organisational, management and communication skills, to play a significant role in the delivery of marine conservation.

- A ☐ have knowledge
- B ☐ provide funding
- C ☐ be instrumental

25.

> The course benefits from the partnership with the Centre for Creative Leadership – in its design and delivery, and from its position as a top global player in leadership development. Its combined format allows candidates to meet .... while studying.

- A ☐ their professional obligations
- B ☐ the high standards expected
- C ☐ all the course requirements

26.

> Watch tonight – Channel 17 at 20^{30} hrs. We need to think about cities in new ways according to economist, Paul Simpson. Simpson debunks the old way of thinking about cities as biological organisms which consume resources and grow in size. But Simpson and his team found that this ....

- A ☐ tells another story
- B ☐ can be clearly verified
- C ☐ is a false metaphor

Test Tip

Identification of the text type will help you. For example, Question 22 is an Internet advert, so B is more likely.

Section 5

Read the passage and complete the sentences below. Put a cross (X) in the box next to the correct answer, as in the example.

Is the best way to motivate people performance-related rewards? Eminent management gurus have been dismissing payment-by-results as simplistic and mechanical, ever since Frederick Taylor tried to turn it into the cornerstone of scientific management in the early 20th century. But there's now a wider debate, sparked by the way bankers and other lavishly remunerated people are paid. In the age of routine production, it made sense for organisations to rely on sticks and carrots, but today, with routine jobs being outsourced or automated, it makes more sense to rely on intrinsic rewards or the pleasure we gain from doing a job well.

Business pundits now maintain that carrots and sticks are not only outdated, but can also be counterproductive – motivation killers and creativity dampeners. Paying people to give blood actually reduces the number who are willing to do so. Providing managers with financial rewards can encourage them to 'game the system' or, even worse, to engage in reckless behaviour.

So how should firms motivate people? Latest theories argue that the answer is to give them more control over their own lives and thus allow them to draw on their deep inner wells of diligence and drive. How convincing is all this? Reviews of research on the subject from the 1980s onwards have all come to the same conclusion: that pay-for-performance can increase productivity dramatically. A study of an American car company, for example, found that shifting from salaries to individual incentives increased productivity by 44%. More recent analysis of workers at a Chinese electronics factory also confirms that performance-related pay, especially the threat of losing income, is an excellent motivator.

Linking pay to performance does not just increase motivation. It also helps to recruit and retain the most talented. The world's brightest students are overwhelmingly attracted to organisations that make extensive use of performance-related rewards, such as partnerships and share options. Firms are adept at using these rewards to encourage long-term loyalty: people work in the salt mines for years in the hope of becoming partners or senior managers. Companies that shun extrinsic rewards risk encumbering themselves with reluctant workers.

Example: The theory that productivity can be stimulated through pay has been

A ☐ scientifically undermined.

B ☐ used successfully up to now.

C ☒ criticised by eminent theorists.

27. More discussion on paying by results
    A ☐ has reached a much wider audience.
    B ☐ has been prompted by reports of high salaries.
    C ☐ has arisen because new business don't believe in it.

28. Today, management experts argue that paying bonuses
    A ☐ works negatively.
    B ☐ is used illegally.
    C ☐ discourages leaders.

29. Investigations into paying for performance demonstrate
    A ☐ that it can improve productivity.
    B ☐ workers respond to other incentives.
    C ☐ employees need greater freedom.

30. Companies have better applicants if they
    A ☐ have a system of large bonuses.
    B ☐ respond to global demands.
    C ☐ offer incentives other than money.

31. If companies don't use any 'carrots', they could
    A ☐ lower morale of low paid workers.
    B ☐ lose their most dedicated staff.
    C ☐ be left with less motivated employees.

Test Tip

Look for paraphrases to locate the answer. For example, in Question 27: "reassessment" matches "there's now a wider debate"; in Question 28: "management experts" matches "business pundits". You are tested on opinions and attitudes; spot the words that indicate these, such as "dismiss, argue, maintain".

Section 6

Read the article below and answer the questions.

IT'S OFTEN COVERT, SELDOM PRETTY AND ALMOST ALWAYS CONTROVERSIAL.
Its perpetrators have been branded as criminals and stars alike. Like it or hate it, street art, or graffiti as it is usually called by opponents, is an urban phenomenon you cannot ignore.

I have always been interested in street art as an urban phenomenon. Most of it is subversive and bordering on the criminal, no doubt, but it can also be an instrument of political and urban commentary. Can it be, in some way, 'controlled' as a device to foster dialogue between the communities that create graffiti and the authorities, rather than as a form of cold war between them? And is the fact that some street art is crossing over towards a more formally recognized form of art in some places, a positive trend with significant cultural and political implications for the city?

I think it is possible – though not without its own set of challenges and limitations – that, handled with the right balance of sensitivity and sternness, a dialogue between authorities and street artists, as representatives of disadvantaged communities in our cities, more often than not, could break the traditional barriers between them.

Example: What do those against graffiti artists label them as?

criminals

32. Where does the writer imply that graffiti is restricted to?

....

33. What type of graffiti is the writer most interested in?

....

34. Which bodies usually fight against graffiti?

....

35. Which section of society do graffiti artists reflect?

....

Test Tip

Generally, the answers you need are words and phrases from the text, so look for equivalent phrasing. For example, in Question 34 "bodies" means the same as "authorities" and "cold war" means the same as "fight".

Section 6 Continued

Read the article below and answer the questions.

Doctor John Membi, a researcher in wildlife trade, argues that there is a proliferation of elephants in some parts of southern Africa. Surplus pachyderms impose a particular burden on the poor, trashing their crops and attacking water sources, children and old people. Culling is sometimes necessary to deal with these problems and, if culling is to happen anyway, the resulting ivory might as well be used to raise some money.

A recent opinion piece in one nature magazine stated baldly that such ivory sales encourage poaching. Dr Membi, however, says the evidence for such a claim is lacking. "We have no baseline data on how much ivory is on the market or what proportion is whale, hippo or bone."

Example: Which group suffers more than most from elephant attacks?

The poor.

36. What, according to Dr Membi, is a logical solution to the problem?

....

37. What is the result of selling ivory according to one source?

....

38. What does the sale of ivory inevitably lead to, according to some?

....

39. What does Dr Membi say is needed before reaching a conclusion?

....

Read the article below and complete the notes that follow. Write no more than three words from the article in each gap.

The revolution in *making books*

Espresso might seem an odd name for a book-making machine. But the wardrobe-sized apparatus at a bookstore in central London and thirty other locations worldwide, can print a paperback in about the time it takes to make and drink a shot of caffeine. A black and white printer produces the pages; a colour one the cover; they are then glued together by a third device.

To some this is just 'retail theatre', a clever way to lure people into bookstores. But others view it as the logical step in a development that has picked up speed recently, yet has not received nearly as much attention as electronic readers or touch-screen tablets: the printing of books on demand, rather than on a publisher's hunch.

It is estimated that about 6% of books in America are now printed on toner-based or inkjet machines – a rough proxy for print-on-demand (POD) – as opposed to on offset presses. It is predicted that this figure will increase to 15%. In 2008, the latest year for which data are available, about 285,000 titles were printed on demand or in short runs – 132% more than in 2007 and, for the first time, more than in the conventional way. Amazon, the world's biggest online bookseller, uses POD machines, although it does not reveal how often.

Better technology is one reason for the rapid growth. These days, only experts can tell whether a book has been printed on an offset machine or a digital one. But economics is the main driver. Estimating the demand and thus the print run for a book has been a guessing game since Gutenberg's day. This means that the industry's supply chain is exceedingly wasteful. About 30% of books in America are returned to the publisher. Although it is still pricier to print books digitally, the overall cost of printing on demand is lower, since books are printed only when there is a buyer, and thus do not languish in a warehouse merely to be destroyed later.

POD has also led to an explosion of self-publishing, allowing authors to bypass sceptical publishers. Authors upload their works free of charge and pay only when they sell a book. Despite all its advantages, POD is unlikely to take over the world. This is because in contrast to digital printing, whose per-unit costs stay pretty much the same, traditional offset printing exhibits strong economies of scale. As long as you have bestsellers with hundreds of thousands of copies, on-demand printing is not going to displace the conventional sort. Then there is regulation. In some countries, such as China, a licence is needed to publish books; others, such as Germany and France, have price controls for books.

Example: There are ...thirty-one.. Espresso machines in operation.

40. The machine produces a book in .... different stages.

41. Some people regard the machine as a .... gimmick.

42. Traditionally books got into print based on ....

43. Figures demonstrate that there is a decline in using .... to produce books.

44. Since the advent of mass-produced books, it has always been difficult to determine

....

45. Printing a book digitally is .... in the long run, unless it is a bestseller.

46. In some circumstances, laws will prevent .... being adopted on a global scale.

Section 8

Use information from Section 7 to help you write your answer.

47. You have read the web article, *The revolution in making books*. Write a response to the article as a blog giving your views. Write about 120–150 words. In your response include:

- information about your own reading habits
- the advantages of printing on demand for authors and readers
- the disadvantages of printing on demand

> **Test Tip**
>
> *150 words is quite short. Write three separate sentences in response to each of the points given, and then build on each to form three separate paragraphs.*

Write your answer here. Do not write outside the box.

Section 9

Choose one of the topics below and write your answer in 200–250 words.

48. A) Pollution

You see an article in your local newspaper about the growing problem of people leaving litter in the streets and the environmental problems caused by plastic carrier bags. The newspaper is asking readers to write follow-up articles.

Write to your local newspaper about this problem suggesting solutions and encourage residents to join you to clean up the town.

Or

48. B) Cities

Write an essay analysing and giving your views on the following statement.

We divide naturally into two groups: those for whom cities are vibrant and exciting, and those for whom they are dirty, noisy and dangerous.

Write your answer here. Do not write outside the box.

Section 10 (2 minutes)

In this section you will speak on your own for about a minute and a half. Listen to what your teacher/examiner asks. Your teacher/examiner will ask one of the main questions below and ask the follow-up questions if necessary.

Main prompt 1:
- Describe a city you have had experience of.

Follow-up prompts:
- What, for you, makes a city a good place to live?
- Which city would you like to visit and why?
- Why do you think there has been such a growth in cities?
- What kind of problems are associated with large cities?

Main prompt 2:
- How concerned are you about the future of the natural world?

Follow-up prompts:
- What do you think are the biggest threats to wildlife?
- What do you or any of your friends do to care for the natural world?
- In what way do you think it's important to save endangered species?
- In what ways are you optimistic about the future of our planet?

Main prompt 3:
- How much do you use new technology in your life?

Follow-up prompts:
- What are the biggest changes for your family in terms of new technologies?
- In what way are there differences in attitudes to technology between older and younger members of your family?
- What should scientists concentrate on to improve life for you or your country?
- What inventions have had a negative effect on the quality of your life?

Main prompt 4:
- What are the qualities of a leader you admire?

Follow-up prompts:
- What motivates you to perform at your best?
- Do you think there are jobs where money is the only motivation for hard work? Why?
- What would you personally have to learn if you wanted to become a good leader?
- What do inspirational leaders have in common?

Test Tip

You are not expected to give a short answer to the question asked. Extend your answers with examples from your own experience.

Section 11 (2 minutes)

In this section you will discuss something with your teacher/examiner.

> **Is too much money spent on advertising?**

What do you think?

Your teacher/examiner will use the following arguments to take an opposing view to yours.

For spending money on advertising:	• Without advertising, companies wouldn't be able to inform the public about what they can buy.
	• The basis of society is buying and selling, so we have to accept advertising.
	• Some advertisements are creative and artistic. Life would be boring without them.
	• Advertisers financially support newspapers, radio, magazines, etc. The quality of these things would go down without advertising.

Against spending money on advertising:	• Some people aren't educated about advertising and believe its claims.
	• We all know that some products are not good for us, but advertising makes people want to buy stuff.
	• The cost of the advertising is passed on to the consumer. It could be reduced and products would be cheaper.
	• It's really annoying to have breaks in TV or radio programmes for advertising.

Test Tip

Don't forget to disagree politely! Learn and use a range of expressions to do this, for example, "That may be true, but ... ." "Don't you think ... ?"

Section 12 (2 minutes)

In this section you will talk for up to 1 minute about two pictures to illustrate audio city guides. They are being considered for an article about such guides, which can be downloaded and taken with you when you visit a city. Tell your teacher/examiner what you can see in the pictures.

Your teacher/examiner will now put this secondary prompt.

Now say which you would choose for the article and why.

Test Tip

At this level, the pictures may represent abstract ideas. Give your opinions and also justify them. For example, "Well, either picture could be used, but I think this picture is more appropriate for an audio guide because ... ."

Section 13 (2 minutes)

In this section you will take part in a role play with your teacher/examiner. Here is a card with the situation and your goal.

TEST TAKER'S CARD

The situation: You have a friend who is thinking of moving from the city to the countryside. You think this is a bad idea.

Your goal: Without offending your friend, persuade him/her to reconsider the idea.

Your teacher/examiner is your friend. Below is a sample script that your teacher/examiner may use.

Ready? I'll start.

You've probably heard I'm thinking of moving to the countryside.

I've dreamed about living in the countryside for a long time.

City life is so busy – I want some peace and quiet.

What I want is a more natural lifestyle.

I know there are advantages to city life but I think I can happily live without them.

That is the end of the test.

Unit Five

The themes for this unit are: social issues/theatre and film/business/advertising

Vocabulary and Grammar

Vocabulary 1: Collocations

Match each word on the left with one from the right and then complete the sentences that follow, as in the example.

ringing	~~encounter~~
thankless	benefit
fundamental	disaster
~~chance~~	coverage
eligibility	endorsement
public	backgrounds
pure	consciousness
media	task
diverse	criteria
natural	shift
potential	theory

Example: Our first meeting was a ..*chance encounter*.. through our shared interest in arts films.

1 Most press releases gave the new play a .... , which should encourage full houses.

2 The company was proud of the fact that it recruited staff from ....

3 There's been a move away from management courses covering just

   ....

4 Although she realised the job was a ...., she knew it had to be done.

5 Of late, the issue of homelessness in our big cities has attracted greater

   ....

6 Volunteers recruited to teach in developing countries face very strict ....

7 There has been a .... in business culture through the availability of 'free' information through the Internet.

8 The speed with which governments take action in the wake of any .... has often been criticised.

9 The documentary showed, perhaps for the first time, that there are .... to living in the slum areas.

10 Since the power of the Internet first came into the .... , businesses have been scrabbling to join in.

Vocabulary 2: Suffixes and prefixes

Complete the following sentences by adding an appropriate prefix and/or suffix to the word in brackets, as in the example.

Example: The company were hampered by the new health and safety regulations although they knew they wouldn't be ..*enforced*.. (FORCE)

1 We are .... to the work of the homeless charities in tackling this social problem. (DEBT)

2 The economic downturn means further investment in research is .... (TENABLE)

3 The rate of growth in Internet advertising over the last few years has been .... (PRECEDENT)

4 The fact that businesses need to think global is not going to change in the .... future. (SEE)

5 He was .... in sticking to his vision of what the film industry needed. (COMPROMISE)

6 He felt it was totally .... to link the failure of the economy to the greed of the banks. (LEAD)

7 He campaigned for solutions to the .... causes of poverty rather than throwing food aid at the problem. (LIE)

8 It appeared a .... exercise to create legislation to prevent hostile takeovers. (POINT)

9 A survey suggests that many firms are guilty of .... the skills that exist in their workforce. (USE)

10 Even today, rates of .... among school leavers are quite shocking. (LITERACY)

Write down the suffixes and prefixes you used above and collect examples of words in which they can be used. Extend your lists with other prefixes and suffixes: *dis ...* , *in ...* , *... ful*, etc.

Grammar 1: Changing the emphasis

Rewrite the following sentences using the beginning given, as in the example.

Example: In the end the producer ran out of cash and the film was never finished.
What ..*happened in the end was that the producer ran out of cash and the film was never finished*.. .

1 We've received a number of complaints about their latest advert.
A number ....

2 What explanation can there be for why he didn't apply for promotion?
Why ever .... ?

3 The food aid finally got through after three weeks.
It ....

4 Although their products appear upmarket, the pricing is reasonable.

Upmarket ....

5 We hadn't been given a clear rationale for the restructuring of the senior team.

What ....

6 A complete apology is the only thing that will satisfy the bank's customers.

Nothing ....

7 The government made efforts to reduce child poverty, but it continued to increase.

In ....

8 The plot of the film is suprising, but the rather obvious ending lets it down.

The thing ....

9 You can try to disguise it, but it's still a financial disaster.

However ....

10 Lack of education is a major cause of poverty in less developed countries.

One ....

Grammar 2: 'If' clauses

Join the two clauses using 'if', making any changes necessary, as in the example. Don't forget to punctuate your sentences.

First clause	Second clause
~~his work been more satisfactory~~	~~he/promote~~
1 investment in training of middle managers seems unrewarding	they/be/not keen to undertake it
2 it can be easy to make over-optimistic forecasts	you/not get/your projections/right
3 you are planning to start a business	documentation systems/be/vital
4 you want to avoid the football	try/watch/the last *Dr Who* film
5 please ring to contact a member of staff	you/wish to use this door
6 your initial proposal meets our eligibility criteria	you/need/to submit a full proposal
7 have money to spend on yourself	how/you/spend it
8 you help me deliver them	I/get the leaflets printed
9 hadn't been to see it already	I/love/to come with you
10 I'd be feeling more relaxed about this	you/manage/to get more quotes

Example: *If his work had been more satisfactory, he would have been promoted* .

1 ....

....

2 ....

....

3 ....

....

4 ....

....

5 ....
....

6 ....
....

7 ....
.... ?

8 ....
....

9 ....
....

10 ....
....

Grammar 3: Modals

Rewrite these sentences using an appropriate modal phrase to replace any underlined words, as in the example. Use one of the following: *should, could, may, would, must*.

Example: <u>I believe</u> everyone loves this type of movie.

Everyone must love this type of movie .

1 <u>It's possible that</u> the contract didn't cover the shipping arrangements.

....

2 The government <u>refused to</u> take any responsibility for the lack of training facilities.

....

3 <u>It really wasn't a good idea</u> to go with the first bank who made you an offer.

....

4 <u>She realised it</u> would have been better if she had consulted her boss.

....

5 <u>It wasn't possible</u> for us to deal with the larger social issues.

....

6 <u>Surely</u> the news alerted you to the fall in the share price.

....

7 <u>I'm sure</u> he wasn't upset just because the funding was going to older directors.

....

8 <u>I'm convinced that</u> he didn't fill in the forms on time to get any unemployment benefit.

....

9 <u>She had the opportunity</u> to become a first-class film director before now.

....

10 His refusal <u>was definitely</u> a sign that his acting days were over.

....

Language skills

⦿ Listening: Listening for the main idea and for specific information

Listen to the recording. What is the main idea of the text?

A The increase in the number of elderly people is an immediate problem.

B The rate of increase in the elderly should be manageable.

C Reported figures on the ratio of the young to the elderly are huge.

Listen again and answer the following questions.

Example: Which body gave the report? *U.S. Bureau*

1 What age does this report focus on? ....

2 Over what period are figures given? ....

3 What is the percentage increase per year in the USA? ....

4 What will the percentage of the elderly be in the UK by 2040? ....

5 Which group in the population is falling in numbers? ....

6 How do workers contribute to the care of the elderly? ....

Speaking: Advertising

Look at the following images and discuss the questions below.

What different impressions do the images convey?
Which image would be most suitable to advertise:

- a sports car?
- washing powder?
- trainers?
- a mobile phone?

What else could these images be used to advertise and how?

Writing: Register

You may be asked in the writing part of the test to write in a formal or informal manner. The message below is an email to a good friend, but it is too formal. Rewrite it in a more informal register.

Dear Jan

You asked how I was progressing. Would it be possible for you to visit me to experience it for yourself? You will be able to imagine it is enormously different from our quiet village. It took me a long time to discover how to get to the university and similarly how to locate where my classes took place on getting there.

I think that the aspect that is most worrying is to understand what coursework is necessary. It's quite confusing, but at least I'm with others in the first year having the same problems. So take care of yourself and it would be lovely if you could come and visit me as I miss you.

Practice Test Five

Section 1

 You will have 10 seconds to read each question and the corresponding options. Then listen to the recording. After the recording you will have 10 seconds to choose the correct option. Put a cross (X) in the box next to the correct answer, as in the example.

Example: The speaker claims that the economies in the developing world

A [X] are moving into new areas of business.

B [ ] no longer rely on cheap labour.

C [ ] need new thinking from entrepreneurs.

---

1. The man

    A [ ] is looking forward to finishing his job.

    B [ ] hasn't decided when he wants to retire.

    C [ ] wants to work until the legal retirement age.

2. The speaker is

    A [ ] motivating pupils to study plays.

    B [ ] describing a university English course.

    C [ ] advertising a literature course for adults.

3. The woman is trying to

    A [ ] confirm.

    B [ ] persuade.

    C [ ] reassure.

4. The speaker is talking about

    A [ ] a choice of TV programmes.

    B [ ] broadcasting live sports events.

    C [ ] the chance to see a superstar.

5. The speaker thinks more attention is needed on issues concerning

    A [ ] recruitment management.

    B [ ] the aging workforce.

    C [ ] keeping young workers.

6. The speaker is
   A ☐ introducing students to an economics course.
   B ☐ describing an advanced course in maths.
   C ☐ explaining a remedial course for school pupils.

7. The writer is saying that she
   A ☐ no longer owns a play once it's written.
   B ☐ expects audiences to respond appropriately.
   C ☐ writes her plays on an emotional level.

8. The male speaker is most likely to be a
   A ☐ TV advertiser.
   B ☐ charity worker.
   C ☐ researcher.

9. The experts are going to discuss the
   A ☐ traditionally accepted role of finance directors.
   B ☐ extending the scope of finance directors' work.
   C ☐ shortcomings of the limited job of finance directors.

10. The man is influenced by the
   A ☐ age of his son's friends.
   B ☐ negative stories he's heard.
   C ☐ distance to school.

Test Tip

At this level, some questions may require you to be able to infer from what the speaker is saying. For example, in Question 1 you are asked to decide what the man is implying and in Question 3 what the woman is trying to do. It is necessary not only to understand the words, but also the function of what is said.

Section 2

You will hear a recording about making films. Listen to the whole recording once. Then you will hear the recording again, with pauses for you to write down what you hear. Make sure you spell the words correctly.

11.

Test Tip

The words which are sometimes the easiest to hear are those which carry the stress, e.g. nouns, verbs, adjectives. It is often more difficult to hear unstressed words like articles, particles and pronouns. When you've finished writing, check these grammatical words. Make sure you haven't missed any.

Section 3

You will hear a radio news item. First, read the notes below, then listen and complete the notes with information from the broadcast.

A recent news item detailed the agreement to give (**Example:**) _20 billion dollars_ to assist countries in the developing world to feed themselves as a better alternative to providing

[12] .... An example of how such projects can be successful is where [13] .... have been trained and funds are used to provide better supplies from seeds to fertiliser. [14] .... suppliers of agricultural products have now been trained. A positive example of the benefits is the much-reduced

[15] .... farmers need to go to buy supplies. Such examples of funding are known as [16] ....

> **Test Tip**
>
> *Listen for the cues which tell you what information is coming up next. Quite often the cues are synonyms of words in the notes. In the example in the first text, the cue is a word meaning the same as "agreement", which is "deal". The cues may not be synonyms, but paraphrases. For example, in Question 13 listen for a paraphrase for "successful projects".*

You will hear a report. First, read the notes below, then listen and complete the notes with information from the report.

> **Example:** Age managers decide to abandon training: _fifty-five_

[17] Suggested focus of training: ....

[18] Recommended timetable of training: ....

[19] Name of enthusiastic trainer: ....

[20] Courses led by: ....

[21] Equipment used: ....

Section 4

Read each text and put a cross (✗) by the missing word or phrase, as in the example.

Example:

This article explores a number of debates which have developed around the significance of 'virtual communities'. This piece examines some of the claims made as to the .... of virtual communities and asks whether they are the democratic, alternative, liberating, safe and effective environments that many claim them to be.

A   ✗   benefits

B   ☐   nature

C   ☐   manner

22.

There is a level access door next to the Theatre Restaurant. A low-level doorbell is provided. Please ring to contact a member of staff if you wish to use this door, as it is not ....
All other entrances to the theatre have some steps.

A   ☐   recommended

B   ☐   manned

C   ☐   signposted

23.

If your initial proposal meets our eligibility criteria, you .... to submit a full proposal. Among eligible proposals, preference will be given to research aimed at developing practical applications of recent scientific knowledge for the benefit of governmental and non-governmental organisations fighting malnutrition.

A   ☐   will be invited

B   ☐   won't need

C   ☐   can choose

24.

ROME THROUGH FILM: presents a study of the worlds created in Roman historical epics. .... analysis of the visual and narrative fabric of seven films set in Ancient Rome, this book demonstrates how cinematic versions of Ancient Rome have been able to captivate us, and inscribe their versions of the city and its history onto our imagination.

A ☐ Studied by
B ☐ Reviewed in
C ☐ Based on

25.

London theatre stalwart, *The Mousetrap* has been extended once again in London's West End, it has been revealed. The play will now have another six months added to its booking period. However, given that the Agatha Christie murder mystery is now in its 58th year in London, it is .... that producers will announce another extension later this year.

A ☐ most disappointing
B ☐ highly likely
C ☐ quite unavoidable

26.

This is a course for graduates who want to work in the marketing communications industry. It is one of the leading courses of its kind in the country. The programme attracts students from all over the world and is delivered over three terms for those ....

A ☐ working in a changing world
B ☐ with strong links in industry
C ☐ studying on a full-time basis

Test Tip

It's important to understand the coherence or logic of each text, which means understanding the complete text, not just the sentence with the gap. For example in Question 25, you need to decide whether the information in the text gives the idea that The Mousetrap *is likely or unlikely to be extended. There are several clues: "once again", "given that", "now in its 58th year".*

Section 5

Read the passage and complete the sentences below. Put a cross (X) in the box next to the correct answer, as in the example.

The Internet is a powerful tool, not only enabling communication between individuals, but also allowing whole groups of people to interact in virtual or 'cyber' space, both private and communal. It can sustain intimate, personal encounters as well as open, accessible forums. Do sociologists have to re-work existing theories of community in order to acknowledge this fundamental shift in the way we construct our relationships?

Since the possibilities afforded by the Internet first entered public consciousness, great claims have been made as to its potential. It is argued that virtual communities allow their members greater freedom, as users are not tied to physical locations. In addition, they free users from the often rigid roles associated with ideas of household, neighbourhood, region or nation, liberating them to communicate in a realm where strictly imposed codes are irrelevant. However, previous communication technologies have worked in similar ways – so how is communication via the Internet fundamentally different? Granted the Internet affords a faster more flexible means of communication, nevertheless, it is another thing to suggest that social relationships shaped through this medium will prove to be fundamentally different.

It has been suggested that those who find each other and communicate on the Internet will engage in 'conversations' which are more focused than those in the physical world. This presupposes that we share an understanding of which encounters convey meaning and significance. All sorts of meetings can be advantageous and rewarding, not only the previously arranged and managed. There are potential benefits and also pleasures associated with chance encounters in shared physical spaces. In real life, one meeting can serve numerous purposes and this can be a strength rather than a limitation.

Vibrant virtual communities seem to hold out the promise of changing the way we communicate, but in reality, many of the problems which plague face-to-face meetings are present in their virtual counterparts. This is hardly surprising given that virtual communities are initiated and maintained by people living in the material world and that users will bring problems, prejudices and limitations into their cyber communities. Despite the tendency for many to herald new technologies as the saviours of society, our future is forged from our past. Most people still find their sources of community in physical spaces. While they may also experiment building networks and friendships across cyberspace, virtual communities have not yet replaced traditional means of building and maintaining community – however flawed these might be.

> **Example:** In the first paragraph the writer
>
> A   ☒   acknowledges the impact of the Internet on how we form relationships.
> B   ☐   questions the work of sociologists on the effects of cyberspace.
> C   ☐   describes how we can use the Internet to create individual groups.

27. The writer challenges the notion that the Internet
    A   ☐   allows users to forget their own culture.
    B   ☐   creates relationships which are exceptional.
    C   ☐   imposes its own rules and regulations.

28. A view the writer refers to in the third paragraph is that Internet relationships
    A   ☐   are not nearly as important as real life ones.
    B   ☐   allow users to concentrate on shared interests.
    C   ☐   can be as satisfying as any other relationship.

29. When people meet by accident in the real world, they
    A   ☐   might have several things in common.
    B   ☐   may have more than one meeting.
    C   ☐   create bonds which last for longer.

30. Which of the following is the best summary of the last paragraph?
    A   ☐   The benefits of the Internet are overstated.
    B   ☐   Technology may change, but people don't.
    C   ☐   People will always have inherent faults.

31. The writer's conclusion is
    A   ☐   communication on the Internet does not require new sociological theories.
    B   ☐   Internet forums are the way forward in establishing communities.
    C   ☐   people behave very differently when they communicate via the Internet.

Test Tip

Remember that some answers might be quite tempting, because they seem to make sense. For example, if you read the questions and the choices without looking at the text, all of them could be possible. However, the questions test your understanding of the information, especially the attitudes and opinions in the text, so always refer to the text and carefully analyse the meaning.

Section 6

Read the article below and answer the questions.

The business-school boom depended largely on the idea that MBAs were entry tickets to the world's two most lucrative professions: investment banking and consultancy. These trades not only consumed more than half the graduates of the leading schools, they also underwrote the schools' finances. Students were willing to pay $100,000 in fees and living expenses (and forgo even more in income) because they were all but guaranteed jobs in these high-paying industries.

But banks and consulting firms are increasingly recruiting people without MBAs, particularly mathematicians and computer scientists. They are also getting keener on growing their own. Why lose a hard-working 25-year-old for a couple of years when you can train him internally and keep him at the coalface? Banks are increasingly dominated by traders who think MBAs are a waste of parchment. Criticism of MBAs extends beyond consultancies and banks. People in many industries worry that business-school professors are more concerned with pure theory than with practical management.

Example: Why have MBAs been so popular?
entry ticket to lucrative professions

32. How many people holding MBAs went into banking and consultancy?

....

33. Why were graduates happy to subsidise MBA courses heavily?

....

34. What is the latest trend instead of MBAs?

....

35. What is the focus of MBA courses leading to dissatisfaction?

....

Section 6 Continued

Read the article below and answer the questions.

The JMK trust presents an annual prize to a young person of outstanding potential, enabling them to mount a full-scale professional production of their choice that they direct. Winning the award has been instrumental in launching the careers of some of Britain's finest new directors. Some contend that too many young theatre directors today studied at prestigious universities like Oxford or Cambridge, but the award's selection process is a rigorous one that encourages applicants from diverse backgrounds.

Recent funding has also allowed the trust to provide a six-month, intensive, mentored training programme throughout the year for eight directors and to expand its remit in 2009 and offer open days providing free, professional workshops at regional theatres. These allowed all those interested in the craft of theatre-making the opportunity to spend time learning from top directors. The first series of five workshops reached 282 participants. It also generated far more applicants for the award than in previous years.

Example: Who is the JMK prize for?

..young theatre directors..

36. What opportunity does winning give?

....

37. Why is the award seen as significant?

....

38. What evidence shows the award isn't elitist?

....

39. How has the trust encouraged a larger number of candidates for their award?

....

Section 7

Read the article below and complete the notes that follow. Write no more than three words from the article in each gap.

Although many of us experience loneliness at one time or another, it is often overlooked or dismissed. Because our society sets great store by self-reliance, loneliness might carry a stigma for people who admit to it.

The Finnish language has a word that means both loneliness and solitude, but the two should not be confused. Many of us live happily alone and get pleasure and satisfaction from solitude. Psychiatrists argue in favour of an introspective approach to life, proposing that solitude is necessary for mental health and creativity, and that the most profound human experiences have little to do with our relationships with others.

However, we're inherently social animals: we're designed to live in close communities and sociology teaches us that we thrive in close co-operation with each other, but our modern way of life increasingly isolates us from others. Some psychologists argue that, as a species, we are unsuited to the physical and social environment we now inhabit. Had a zookeeper been asked to construct an enclosure suitable for man, his instructions would have warned him of the social nature of our species. Instead, more of us live alone in small apartments, work at home, and shop and socialise online. Or we commute long distances back and forth to work long hours at the office, barely finding time to spend with our families.

In modern times, electronic communication appears to be keeping many of us connected. In a recent survey, two thirds (62%) of the respondents say technology helps them stay in touch with those they might otherwise lose touch with. While not face-to-face, it is likely to be better than no communication at all, especially for those living far away from friends and loved ones. The results also support evidence that increasing numbers of people are moving away from their roots. Because of careers or education, more of us live further from our families and the communities we grew up in.

Behind such statistics are demographic changes and lifestyle choices. But shifts in attitude also play a part: today, socialising and investing time in social ties are generally seen as less important than 'productive' activities like work. A 'cult of busyness' has become a modern badge of honour. Researchers suggest that we face so much pressure to be 'productive' that we neglect 'unnecessary' relationships that are as vital as food and water. Long working hours are frequently cited as having a negative impact on family life. For many people, working long hours is a necessity to support their families, rather than a choice.

Example: Loneliness is neglected because people today value _self-reliance_ .

40. Some academics maintain that .... is an indispensable aspect of well-being.

41. Modern life has developed in a way that ignores the .... of humans.

42. A large number of people make contact through ....

43. People leave their hometown or village for ....

44. The results of the survey can be partly explained by changes in ....

45. Devoting energy to .... is considered secondary to work.

46. To appear to be always .... is like a new religion.

Section 8

Use information from Section 7 to help you write your answer.

47. You have read the article. Write an email to a good friend. Write about 120–150 words. In your email you should include:

- your views on whether modern life can lead to loneliness
- whether you agree with the attitudes to work described in the article
- your suggestions on how you'll make sure you have a work/life balance

Write your answer here. Do not write outside the box.

Section 9

Choose one of the topics below and write your answer in 200–250 words.

> **Test Tip**
>
> *Check the type of text required. The most common are: essay, article, report and review. Use effective linking words or expressions so the reader can follow the function of each sentence. For example: "In my opinion …", "An illustration of this is …", "However, …" etc.*

48. A) Business and commerce

You see the following on the Fairtrade website:

Fairtrade is about better prices, decent working conditions, local sustainability, and fair terms of trade for farmers and workers in the developing world.

Write a report for your college magazine urging the purchase of Fairtrade products.

Or

48. B) Cinema

A local group is campaigning to save your local cinema from closure. **Write a blog entry for the campaigners' website supporting the group.**

Write your answer here. Do not write outside the box.

Section 10 (2 minutes)

In this section you will speak on your own for about a minute and a half. Listen to what your teacher/examiner asks. Your teacher/examiner will ask one of the main questions below and ask the follow-up questions if necessary.

Main prompt 1:
- In what way are you concerned about people in countries poorer than yours?

Follow-up prompts:
- What do you do to help people in need?
- Which charities would you like to help and why?
- How do you think governments should help poorer countries?
- What issues are the most pressing globally in your view?

Main prompt 2:
- How important are the theatre or films in your life?

Follow-up prompts:
- What was the most memorable film or play you have seen? Why?
- How influential is having a megastar in a film in persuading you to watch it?
- How much do you discuss films or plays with your friends?
- How far do you think films and plays have a social role?

Main prompt 3:
- If you have money to spend on yourself, how do you spend it?

Follow-up prompts:
- How do you decide to spend your money?
- Do you think buying things over the Internet is a good or bad thing? Why?
- What advice would you give to young people today about spending money?
- What in your view are the best and worst aspects of capitalism?

Main prompt 4:
- In what ways do you and your friends use modern technology?

Follow-up prompts:
- How do the older generation in your family use modern technology?
- Do you think today's technology creates any social issues?
- How would you be affected if mobile phones were banned?
- Why do you think some people call themselves 'technophobes'?

Test Tip

In the first part of the spoken test, you are expected to talk about personal experiences, interests, tastes and attitudes for at least one and a half minutes. This is quite a long time, so be prepared to give examples from your own experience. You can always preface such anecdotes with expressions such as, "This may not be a good example of what you mean, but … ." Remember the examiner is not looking for the right answer, but how you can express yourself in English.

Section 11 (2 minutes)

In this section you will discuss something with your teacher/examiner.

> **Is it easier nowadays to be friends with people from different countries?**

What do you think?

Your teacher/examiner will use the following arguments to take an opposing view to yours.

For making friends more easily:	• People move around much more and so they can meet people from different countries and backgrounds more easily. • We are much better educated now and have fewer prejudices. • The whole class system where people only had friends from the same culture and background has broken down. • The Internet allows us to make friends with people from different countries and different backgrounds more easily.

Against making friends more easily:	• We still prefer to be with people who share the same values. • Prejudice against certain classes and cultures still exists. • It is natural for people to stick together with people from the same background. • Friendships made on the Internet are only superficial.

> **Test Tip**
>
> *In this part of the test you will demonstrate your ability to exchange opinions. Don't forget to ask the examiner questions: "What do you mean exactly? What makes you think that? How can you be so sure?" This will make it a two-way discussion.*

Section 12 (2 minutes)

In this section you will talk for up to 1 minute about these two pictures. The pictures are being considered for an advertisement for a film school. Tell your teacher/examiner what you can see in the pictures.

Your teacher/examiner will now put this secondary prompt.

Now say which one you would choose for the advertisement and why.

Section 13 (2 minutes)

In this section you will take part in a role play with your teacher/examiner. Here is a card with the situation and your goal.

TEST TAKER'S CARD

The situation: Your friend has just started their own business and wants your advice about advertising. You think the best idea is to do a leaflet drop in the area because people keep leaflets.

Your goal: To persuade your friend to use a leaflet drop.

Your teacher/examiner has just started their own business and wants to advertise to get customers. Advise him/her on what to do. Below is a sample script that your teacher/examiner may use.

Ready? I'll start.

What do you think I should do to get customers?

Well, I thought it would be better to have a web page.

Everybody uses the Internet these days.

I haven't got time to deliver loads of leaflets.

Anyway, what about the cost of printing?

I don't think it's the best way. Perhaps I should advertise in the local paper.

I tell you what, I'll do the leaflet drop if you help me.

Test Tip

Check carefully what your goal is. If it is to persuade, make sure you use appropriate language: "I really think you should ... , Why don't you ... , It would be better if you ... ."

That is the end of the test.

Writing guide

Introduction

Writing tasks in the Pearson Test of English General

In the Pearson Test of English General test, there are two sections which assess your writing skills.

Section 8

In this section you are asked to write a piece of correspondence. This may take the form of a letter, an email or another form of electronic communication such as a contribution to a web page.

What you have to write will always be a response to the text you read in Section 7. For example, you may be asked to respond to a newspaper story by writing a letter to the newspaper. You will need to refer to the text in the previous section, usually by summarising the main idea and/or commenting on it. In either case, you should use your own words as far as possible, not simply copy parts of the original text. Exactly what you need to include is indicated by three bullet-pointed instructions.

The word limit in this section is 120–150 words. You may well find that the biggest problem is not that this is a lot of words but that, once you start writing, it is not enough to include everything that you want. For this reason it is important to express yourself concisely.

Section 9

This section is a free writing task in which you will need to express your point of view, explain the advantages and disadvantages of something or develop an argument. What you are asked to write can take various forms. It may be something factual (for example a leaflet or article), critical (for example a review or report) or analytical (for example an essay).

There will be a choice of two tasks. The topics will be related to two of the themes of the test so there may be ideas in other sections, but again you should use your own words. The word limit is 200–250 words.

General advice

There are specific tips in the relevant test sections of this book. Below are some more general pieces of advice relating to writing in general and in the Pearson Test of English General test.

- Always be aware of the reader, the person or people that you are writing for. This will have an effect on both the content and the style/register of what you write. Generally speaking, an informal, more conversational style is best for letters and emails to friends and for light-hearted articles, while a semi-formal or neutral style is better for more serious articles or essays.

- Don't try to be over-ambitious and use superficially "impressive" language, especially if you're unsure about it. This may be a higher level test but the true sign of a good writer is the <u>appropriate</u> use of language, not its complexity. If you're not sure how to say something in English, either say it in a simpler way or say something else.

- Don't pre-learn large sections and long phrases, for example introductions, and try to fit them into your writing, whatever the topic. Firstly, it often looks unnatural and is usually easy for the examiner to notice. Secondly, it is often a waste of words: if you use a lot of words on "decoration", you might find you have no room left to say anything useful.

- Make a short plan of what you want to write. In this way your writing will be clearer, more coherent and better organised. Paragraphing makes the organisation of your writing clear. Linking words and phrases will also help to do this, but if the writing is well organised, it does not need very many. It is probably enough to have two or three basic words or phrases for various purposes, for example *and*, *also* and *in addition* for adding extra information or *but*, *whereas* and *however* for showing contrast. The most important thing is that you understand how to use them.

- When you have finished writing, check what you have written for mistakes, especially the ones you make under pressure that you would get right if you thought about it. Try to be aware of the kinds of mistake you tend to make frequently.

- Your writing will be marked for how well it performs the task as well as for the language, so make sure you cover all the points required by the question and bullet points.

Letters to magazines or newspapers

Model answer

You have read an article about the importance of eating healthy food and the dangers of 'junk food' on our health. Write a letter to the newspaper saying why it may be difficult for many people to follow this advice. Write about 120-150 words.

- Say why you think the basic idea in the article is a good idea.
- Describe some reasons why it may not be so easy for some people.
- Say what supermarkets and fast-food restaurants could do to help.

Using a linking word like *although* is a good way of setting up a contrasting idea, or for giving a reason for why something might not be as straightforward as is suggested.

Using an expression like this: *for many people it isn't so simple ...* , prepares the reader for some examples or reasons to follow. So it's a useful way to make them want to read more.

Starting a sentence with *What* ... again raises the level of anticipation in the reader. As soon as he/she reads *What your article fails to mention is ...* , he/she knows that another key point is about to be made.

> Dear Sir/Madam,
>
> I found your article about healthy food interesting, but I think you failed to discuss some very important issues. Everyone knows about the dangers of eating unhealthy food, but although we get lots of advice about healthy diets, for many people it isn't so simple to suddenly start a diet of good food. They may be very busy and not have time to think enough about the food they eat. They may find it easier to buy a pizza or a hamburger. They may find healthy food too expensive.
> What your article fails to mention is that we still find 'junk food' in attractive packets in supermarkets. We still find fast-food restaurants everywhere. They should help us become more healthy by selling good quality food which is quick to prepare and cheap to buy.
> Yours,
>
> _____
> [138 words]

The first sentence should get straight to the point by referring to the context, identifying yourself (if necessary) and stating your reason for writing. This particular sentence construction is a very useful way of beginning a letter like this because you can introduce your letter on a positive note and then add *but* to prepare the reader for some different views.

Lists in threes are a very effective construction and make a point forcefully in writing of this kind. Also, the repetition of *they may* reinforces the point.

Note the use of the cohesive device *by* in this sentence, which is used to introduce ways in which supermarkets and fast-food restaurants can improve the situation.

Practice

1 You read an article in a newspaper about the violence depicted in computer games. The writer obviously thinks that there is too much violence shown in these games and that this could damage young people in some way. Write a letter to the magazine giving your own view on the review. Write about 120–150 words.

2 You read a review in your local newspaper about a new restaurant in your town. The review is very critical of the food and the service. You went to the same restaurant this week and found everything very good. Write a response to the review stating your own view and criticising the critic. Write about 120–150 words.

Emails and other forms of electronic communication
Model answer

You read a discussion on a website entitled 'Why we don't need books any more', about how our access to technology is replacing the need for books.

Write a contribution to the website, giving your opinion. Write about 120–150 words.

There are lots of different ways of announcing your opinion in a piece of writing. Here the writer uses *to my mind*, but could also use *as far as I'm concerned* or *in my opinion*.

Here is an example of someone giving a very strong opinion: *the truth is ...* , implies that there is no discussion, it's a fact. Be careful if you decide to use this kind of language. It can emphasise a point, but should be used sparingly. Other examples are: *it is the case that ...* , *it's absolutely sure that ...* , *what I am certain about is ...* .

These kinds of phrases are used to link two ideas within the same subject matter. Imagine how abrupt or sudden the change to talking about novels would be if the phrase *and while we are on the subject of ...* were not there.

Yes, of course, nowadays we can find as much information as we need on the Internet. But to my mind, books do much more than simply give us information. Whether we are talking about fiction or non-fiction, the truth is that a book provides the background to a story, explores its history and its characters and allows the author to express and develop a point of view.

A book is real; it's there; you can turn its pages, pick it up, hold it, flick through its pages, check back to an earlier page. You might argue that the Internet can do all these things but somehow it's not the same. And while we are on the subject of books, you will never replace a good novel with technology. It is something so deep in our culture that I don't believe it will ever die.
[144 words]

You have a limited number of words, so it's important to get straight to the point. In the opening sentence, the writer manages to briefly summarise the point he/she is responding to, whilst at the same time preparing the reader for an alternative point of view.

The use of short, sharp and simple phrases is a very powerful way of making your point strongly. In this case the writer is almost making a list and repeats the pronoun *it* to refer to the book. This is an especially effective approach when the short phrases are followed by a longer phrase or sentence to provide contrast.

Practice

1 You read a discussion forum on a media website comparing the experience of watching films on DVD and watching them at the cinema. Write a contribution to the debate giving your views on the two forms of watching movies. Write about 120–150 words.

2 You read an article on a website saying that technology will soon replace newspapers. The website asks readers to add their opinion and give examples. Write your contribution in about 120–150 words.

Essays

Model answer

You have been asked to write an essay in answer to the following question.
Is higher education worth it?
Many students make the decision not to do a university course and to get a full-time job when they finish school, even if their results are good enough to continue their academic education. Are they doing the right thing? What are the advantages and disadvantages of this decision?
Write about 200–250 words.

Note that the second half of the sentence explains the first. In this case the word *when* is used instead of *because* or *as a result of.*

Use these kinds of devices when you want to develop a list of examples or ideas: *first of all … , secondly … , finally … .* Other simple sequences like this is are: *in the first place … , to begin with … , then … , next … ,* etc. But make sure that, when you use these, you continue the sequence. If you write *firstly … ,* make sure you then have a *secondly … ,* otherwise you will lose your readers.

It's always useful to personalise your writing by giving examples of your own experience as it relates to the subject matter. Most of the topics presented are those which have some relevance to your own life so you will be able to do this.

Conclude the essay by referring back to the question and giving your own opinion.

Is higher education worth it?
Most people would say that, if you have the ability, then you should continue with your academic education after you finish school. Getting good qualifications is important today, when it is getting more and more difficult to get a job. But there are several disadvantages. First of all, it's expensive. Apart from the fees you (or your parents) may have to pay, you also spend at least three years of your life not earning money. So who is going to support you? Many children of less wealthy parents simply can't afford to pay the fees, so they get a job. Secondly, there is no guarantee that you get a job when you finish. Graduate unemployment is becoming more and more widespread.
It's true to say that academic education suits some people, while other people benefit more from the practical experience of getting a job rather than doing more study. Many jobs these days include training programmes for that specific job so the education is more focused. In my own experience, I was undecided what I wanted to do when I left school, but I eventually thought that the opportunity to go to university was too good to miss as you get an education and you meet interesting people. But I didn't simply choose an interesting academic subject. Instead I chose a practical subject which would improve my chances of employment when I finished university.
So I would say that, yes, higher education is definitely worth it if you use it carefully to give yourself a good chance of using it to find employment.
[262 words]

Don't waste words by repeating the question. Get straight into answering the question by using expressions like the one used here: *Most people would say … .* Then you can elaborate and develop your own argument without wasting any words.

These are known as rhetorical questions. They are asked to make a point rather than find out information so they don't expect an answer. Questions like this are typical in spoken arguments but they can also be used in written contexts. As with all such figures of speech, however, they should not be overused.

So is a cohesive device linking the first part of the sentence, which states the problem, with the second part of the sentence, which gives a possible solution. We could rewrite the sentence like this: *Because many … can't afford to pay the fees, they get a job.* But it is more effective to use *so.* Think of it as meaning *as a result.*

Practice

Write an essay in answer to the following questions in about 200–250 words.
1 Do you think famous sports personalities get paid too much? Give some examples and give reasons for your answer.
2 "Cheap travel will soon be a thing of the past and holidays will never be the same again." Why do you think this statement has been made and how far do you agree with it?

Articles

Model answer

You have agreed to write an article for your school/college magazine, which is producing a special edition entitled "Youth Today".

Write about 200–250 words.

The first sentence is important as you want to spark the readers' interest and get them to read further. You can do this in different ways. In this example the writer apparently agrees that life should be better, but by including *in many ways* in the first line, prepares the reader for the opposite view.

Another example of a rhetorical question, which makes a point, rather than expecting an answer and prepares the reader for some examples.

Another example of repetitive language to present a list of items or ideas for effect.

This is a useful device for writing for effect. In this case there is a list of things we want to acquire and at the end we are brought down suddenly by the simple sentence *and that costs money.*

Are youngsters today happier than they were 50 years ago?

In many ways, it's true to say that life is better for many people today. Technology, science and medicine have made our lives easier, safer and healthier, the age of cheap travel has allowed us to see places we could have only dreamt about fifty years ago, and music and film are much more available.

If that is the case, why is there so much stress in modern life? The same technology and media that have improved so many aspects of our lives, are also responsible for making us anxious. We are constantly exposed to people telling us what we should look like, what we should be wearing, what we should be listening to, what phone we should be using. We see our idols on the TV and want to be like them. We have to have the best, the newest, the most fashionable – and that costs money.

There is also much more pressure in the workplace. Years ago, you would finish your education and get a job you could stay in as long as you wanted. But now you get a job and before you know it, people are telling you that you have to move on. It seems there is no such thing as a permanent job any more.

So are youngsters happier now than fifty years ago? Despite all the excitement and the fast pace of life today, I really don't think they are. If you're one of the young people affected, you'll probably never know.

[250 words]

Articles usually have a title or a heading to attract the reader's attention. This is not absolutely necessary but including one will make your article look more realistic and create a good impression from the start.

This series of clauses expands on the areas that have helped improve our lives in recent years.

The use of two contrasting sentences to make a point is very effective in this kind of writing.

This last short paragraph returns to the question originally asked and attempts to answer it.

Practice

1 You see this advertisement in an English language magazine and decide to write an article and enter the competition.

PRIZES TO BE WON

Our writing competition this month is entitled

'An experience that changed my life'.

Write an essay describing your experience and say why you think it changed your life.

Write an article in about 200–250 words.

2 You see this notice in your college magazine.

✓ **"The best way to study"**

We need articles for the next issue
to help new students coming to the college.
Tell us your "top tips" on how to study effectively
and which work for you so we
can pass them on to others.

Write an article in about 200–250 words.

Glossary

Unit 1

alienation (n) the feeling of not being part of society or a group

allergy (n) a medical condition in which you become ill or in which your skin becomes red and painful because you have eaten or touched a particular substance

allowance (n) an amount of money that you are given regularly or for a special purpose

audacious (adj) showing great courage or confidence in a way that is impressive or slightly shocking

bassoon (n) a musical instrument like a very long wooden tube, that produces a low sound. You play it by blowing into a thin curved metal pipe

bitten by (adj) have a very strong interest in something, for example a hobby

blackmail (n) when someone tries to get money from you or make you do what they want by telling other people your secrets

blare out (phr v) to make a very loud unpleasant sound

bloodstream (n) the blood flowing in your body

blueprint (n) a plan for achieving something; a photographic plan of a building, machine, etc.

boom (n) an increase in how popular or successful something is, or in how often it happens

bug (n) a sudden strong interest in doing something

cardiologist (n) a doctor who studies or treats heart diseases

catchy (adj) a catchy tune or phrase is one that is easy to remember

cello (n) a musical instrument like a large violin that you hold between your knees and play by pulling a bow across the strings

choppy (adj) choppy water has a lot of waves and is not smooth to sail on

clarinet (n) a musical instrument like a long black tube that you play by blowing into it and pressing keys to change the notes

come through (phr v) to continue to live, be strong or succeed after a difficult or dangerous time

come to a head (v phr) if a problem or difficult situation comes to a head, or something brings it to a head, it suddenly becomes worse and has to be dealt with swiftly

crack of dawn (n) very early in the morning

deadline (n) a date or time by which you have to do or complete something

debilitate (v) to make someone ill or weak; to make an organisation or system less effective or powerful

disorder (n) a mental or physical illness which prevents part of your body from working properly

double bass (n) a very large musical instrument shaped like a violin that the musician plays standing up

download (v) to move information or programs from a computer network to a small computer

expectancy (n) the feeling that something pleasant or exciting is going to happen

gene (n) a part of a cell in a living thing that controls what it looks like, how it grows, and how it develops

genetics (n) the study of how the qualities of living things are passed on in their genes

get on with (phr v) to continue doing something

get somewhere (v phr) to make progress

go on about (phr v) to talk too much about

gratification (n) a feeling of being pleased and satisfied

inception (n) the start of an organisation or institution

jolt (n) a sudden shock

laptop (n) a small computer that you can carry with you

laze (v) to relax and enjoy yourself in a lazy way

lyrics (n pl) the words of a song

movement (n) one of the main parts into which a piece of music is divided, especially a symphony

niggle (v) if something niggles you, you keep worrying about it or feeling annoyed about it and you cannot forget about it

obesity (n) when someone is very fat in a way that is unhealthy

opening (n) a job that is available

overdo it (v) to work too hard or be too active so that you become tired

overstep the mark (v phr) to offend someone by doing or saying things that you should not do or say

pay off (phr v) if something you do pays off, it is successful or has a good result

perk (n) something that you get legally from your work in addition to your wages, such as goods, meals or a car

pet hate (n) something that you strongly dislike because it always annoys you

pick up (phr v) to acquire, win or collect something

pitch (n) how high or low a note or other sound is

plough on (phr v) to continue doing something that is difficult or boring

plummet (v) to suddenly and quickly decrease in value or amount

propel (v) to move someone into a new situation or make them do something

pull one's weight (v phr) to do your full share of work, etc.

pursuit (n) an activity such as a sport or hobby, which you spend a lot of time doing

put through (phr v) to make someone do or experience something difficult or unpleasant

rake (n) a gardening tool with a row of metal teeth at the end of a long handle, used for making soil level, gathering up dead leaves, etc.

regime (n) a special plan of food, exercise, etc. that is intended to improve your health

repercussions (n pl) the effects of an action or event, especially bad effects that continue for some time

sea change (n) a very big change in something

status symbol (n) something that you have or own that you think shows high social rank or position

stick to (phr v) to do or keep doing what you said you would do or what you believe in, even when it is difficult

stick together (phr v) if people stick together, they continue to support each other when they have problems

suit yourself (v phr) used to tell someone they can do whatever they want to, even though it annoys you or you think they are not doing the right thing

surround sound (n) a system of four or more speakers used so that sound from a film or television programme comes from all directions

time off (n) time when you are officially allowed not to be at work or studying

tone (n) the quality of a sound, especially the sound of a musical instrument or someone's voice

trigger (v) to make something happen very quickly, especially a series of events

undergo (v) if you undergo a change, an unpleasant experience, etc., it happens to you or is done to you

unspecified (adj) not known or not stated

venue (n) a place where an organized meeting, concert, etc. takes place

viola (n) a wooden instrument that you play like a violin but that is larger and has a lower sound

violin (n) a small wooden musical instrument that you hold under your chin and play by pulling a bow across the strings

vocational (adj) teaching or relating to the skills you need to do a particular job

whine (v) to complain in a sad, annoying voice about something

whittle down (phr v) to gradually make something smaller by taking parts away

Unit 2

accountable (adj) responsible for the effects of your actions and willing to explain or be criticized for them

accumulate (v) to gradually get more money, possessions, knowledge, etc. over a period of time; to gradually increase in numbers or amount

allergen (n) a substance that causes an allergy

allergy (n) a medical condition in which you become ill or in which your skin becomes red and painful because you have eaten or touched a particular substance

anger management (n) the ability to control one's anger

answerable to (adj) having to explain one's actions to someone in authority

anxious (adj) worried about something

apathetic (adj) not interested in something, and not willing to make any effort to change or improve things

apathy (n) the feeling of not being interested in something, and not willing to make any effort to change or improve things

attain (v) to succeed in achieving something after trying for a long time

balance of payments (n) the difference between what a country spends in order to buy goods and services abroad and the money it earns selling goods and services abroad

borrow (v) to take and use something that belongs to someone else and that you must give back to them later

borrower (n) someone who borrows, especially money from a bank or books from a library

bound to (adv) very likely to do or feel something

brand (v) to describe someone or something as a very bad type of person or thing, often unfairly

breakdown (n) a serious medical condition in which someone becomes mentally ill and unable to work or deal with ordinary situations in life

browse (v) to look through the pages of a book, magazine, etc. without a particular purpose; to look at the goods in a shop without wanting to buy any particular thing

bygone (adj) of a period of time in the past

bypass (n) a road that goes around a town or other busy area rather than through it

cheat (v) to behave in a dishonest way in order to win or get an advantage, especially in a competition, game or examination

complacent (adj) pleased with a situation, especially something you have achieved, so that you stop trying to improve or change things

compound (v) to make a difficult situation worse by adding more problems

corrupt (adj) using your power in a dishonest or illegal way in order to get an advantage for yourself

counselling (n) advice and support given by a counsellor to someone with problems, especially after talking to them

counteract (v) to reduce or prevent the bad effect of something by doing something that has the opposite effect

cover up (phr v) to prevent people from discovering mistakes or unpleasant facts

culminate (v) if a process culminates in or with a particular event, it ends with that event

depression (n) a medical condition that makes you very unhappy and anxious and often prevents you from living a normal life

disengagement (n) stopping being involved or interested in something

disillusion (v) to make someone realize that something that they thought was true or good is not really true or good

distress (n) a feeling of extreme unhappiness

draft (n) a piece of writing that is not yet in its finished form

endurance (n) the ability to continue doing something difficult or painful over a long period of time

engagement (n) when you become involved with someone or something in order to understand them

equate with (phr v) to consider that two things are similar or connected

escalate (v) if fighting, violence or a bad situation escalates, it becomes much worse

exposure (n) the attention that someone or something gets from newspapers, television, etc.

extravagant (adj) spending or costing a lot of money, especially more than is necessary or more than you can afford

feminise (v) to change something so that it includes women, is suitable for women, or is considered typical of women

flourishing (adj) very successful, growing well

fly off the handle (phr) to suddenly get very angry

folder (n) a group of related documents that you store together on a computer

gland (n) an organ of the body which produces a substance that the body needs such as hormones, sweat

grieve (v) to feel extremely sad, especially because someone you love has died

heyday (n) the time when someone or something was most popular, successful or powerful

hormone (n) a chemical substance produced by your body that influences its growth, development and condition

ill-considered (adj) decisions, actions, ideas, etc. that are ill-considered have not been carefully thought about

impenetrable (adj) very difficult or impossible to understand

ingredient (n) one of the foods that you use to make a particular food or dish

inherent (adj) a quality that is inherent in something is a natural part of it and cannot be separated from it

initiative (n) the ability to make decisions and take actions without waiting for someone to tell you what to do; an important new plan or process to solve a particular problem

issue (n) a subject or problem that is often discussed or argued about, especially a social or political matter that affects the interests of a lot of people

kid (n) a child or young person

know-how (n) knowledge, practical ability, or skill to do something

layout (n) the way in which something such as a town, garden or building is arranged

lower (v) to reduce something in amount, degree, strength, level, etc.

mistrust (n) the feeling that you cannot trust someone, especially because you feel that they may treat you unfairly or dishonestly

mite (n) a very small creature that lives in plants, carpets, etc.

narrator (n) the person who tells the story in a book or a play

nominate (v) to officially suggest someone or something for an important position, duty or prize

operator (n) someone who is good at achieving things by persuading people to help or agree with them

opposition (n) in some countries such as Britain, the main political party in the parliament that is not part of the government

outgrow (v) to no longer do or enjoy something that you used to do, because you have grown older and changed

output (n) the amount of goods or work produced by a person, machine, factory, etc.

pastime (n) something that you do because you think it is interesting or enjoyable

petition (n) a written request signed by a lot of people, asking someone in authority to do something or change something

populist (adj) related to or representing ordinary people, rather than rich or very highly-educated people

predecessor (n) someone who had your job before you started doing it

productivity (n) the rate at which goods are produced, and the amount produced, especially in relation to the work, time and money needed to produce them

promising (adj) showing signs of being successful or good in the future

protester (n) someone who takes a part in a public activity such as a demonstration in order to show their opposition to something

provocative (adj) provocative remarks, behaviour, etc. are intended to make people angry or upset, or to cause a lot of discussion

purpose (n) the purpose of something is what it is intended to achieve

reasoning (n) a process of thinking carefully about something in order to make a judgement

relax (v) to rest or do something that is enjoyable, especially after you have been working

revert to (phr v) to change back to a situation that existed in the past

run (v) to try to be elected in an election

ruthless (adj) so determined to get what you want that you do not care if you have to hurt other people in order to do it

scandal (n) an event in which someone, especially someone important, behaves in a bad way that shocks people

set in (v) if something sets in, especially something unpleasant, it begins and seems likely to continue for a long time

shut away (phr v) to put someone or something in a place away from other people where they cannot be seen

soul (n) the part of a person that is not physical, and that contains their character, thoughts and feelings

stack up (phr v) to make things into a neat pile

stain (v) something that damages the good opinion that people have about someone

straight talking (adj) honest and direct, always telling the truth

strain (n) a difficulty or problem that is caused when a person, relationship, organization or system has too much to do or too many problems to deal with

strike (n) a period of time when a group of workers deliberately stop working because of a disagreement about pay, working conditions, etc.

susceptible (adj) likely to suffer from a particular illness or be affected by a particular problem

tear jerker (n) a film, book or story that is very sad and makes you cry

therapist (n) someone who has been trained to give a particular form of treatment for physical or mental illness

touchy-feely (adj) too concerned with feelings and emotions, rather than with facts or actions

turn (n) the time when it is your chance, duty or right to do something that each person in a group is doing one after the other

unfeeling (adj) not sympathetic towards other people's feelings

upholstery (n) material that is used to cover chairs

uplift (v) to make someone feel happier; to make something higher

whopping (adj) very large

witty (adj) using words in a clever and amusing way

Unit 3

abide by (phr v) to accept and obey a decision, rule, agreement, etc., even though you may not agree with it

appalled (adj) very shocked and upset by something very bad or unpleasant

around the clock (phr) all day and night, without stopping

authoritative (adj) an authoritative book, account, etc. is respected because the person who wrote it knows a lot about the subject; behaving or speaking in a confident, determined way that makes people respect and obey you

be up to (phr v) be clever, good or well enough to do something

bums on seats (n pl) the number of people, usually a large number, who go to see a film, play, sports match, etc.

be burdened with (v phr) to have a lot of problems because of a particular thing

catch someone's eye (v phr) to look at someone at the same moment that they are looking at you; to attract someone's attention and make them look at something

catch up (phr v) to improve and reach the same standard as other people in your class, group, etc.

character building (adj) designed or meant to improve someone's strong qualities

chartered (adj) qualified according to the rules of a professional organization that has a royal charter

civil (adj) polite in a formal but not very friendly way

con (n) a trick to get someone's money or make them do something

deceit (n) behaviour that is intended to make someone believe something that is not true

delivery (n) the way in which someone speaks in public

detractor (n) someone who says bad things about someone or something in order to make them seem less good than they really are

distort (v) to report something in a way that is not completely true or correct

distract (v) to take someone's attention away from something by making them look at or listen to something else

divorce (n) the legal ending of a marriage

downfall (n) something that causes a complete failure or loss of someone's money, moral standards, social position, etc.

drudgery (n) hard boring work

employable (adj) having skills or qualities that are necessary to get a job

estimate (v) to try to judge the value, size, speed, cost, etc. of something, without calculating it exactly

extrovert (n) someone who is active and confident, and who enjoys spending time with other people

flash (n) a sudden, very brief event

forefront (n) the leading position in an important activity that is trying to achieve something or develop new ideas

get ahead (phr v) be successful and do better than other people in a job or work

greedy (adj) always wanting more food, money, power, possessions, etc. than you need

hand over (phr v) to give someone power or responsibility over something that you used to be in charge of

icing on the cake (phr) something that makes a very good experience even better

immunity (n) the state or right of being protected from particular laws or from unpleasant things; the state of being immune to a disease

imply (v) to suggest that something is true, without saying this directly

infer (v) to form an opinion that something is probably true because of information that you have

interact (v) if people interact with each other, they talk to each other, work together, etc.

introvert (n) someone who is quiet and shy, and does not enjoy being with other people

lack (v) to not have something that you need, or not have enough of it

lucid (adj) able to understand and think clearly, used especially about someone who is not always able to do this

measured (adj) if you do something in a measured way, you do it in a careful and controlled way, not in an excited or sudden way

mislead (v) to make someone believe something that is not true by giving them information that is false or not complete

miss out (phr v) to not have the chance to do something that you enjoy and that would be good for you

mix-up (n) a mistake that causes confusion about details or arrangements

mortality (n) the condition of being human and having to die

offset (v) if the cost or amount of something offsets another cost or amount, the two things have an opposite effect so that the situation remains the same

open-minded (adj) willing to consider and accept other people's opinions and ideas

pass on (phr v) to give something, especially a disease, to your children through your genes

pattern (n) a regularly repeated arrangement of shapes, colours or lines on a surface, usually as a decoration

portrayal (n) the way someone or something is described or shown in a book, film, play, etc.

poverty-stricken (adj) extremely poor

pressing (adj) needing to be discussed or dealt with very soon

prospects (n pl) chances of success in the future

rabies (n) a very dangerous disease that affects dogs and other animals, and that you can catch if you are bitten by an infected animal

rival (n) a person, group or organization that you compete with in sport, business, a fight, etc.

run out (phr v) to use all of something and not have any more left

school leaver (n) someone who has just left school, especially to do or look for a job rather than going to college, university, etc.

site (n) a place that is used for a particular purpose

slum (n) a house or an area of a city that is in very bad condition, where very poor people live

solitary (adj) spending a lot of time alone, usually because you like being alone

stature (n) the degree to which someone is admired or regarded as important

stay on (phr v) to continue to do a job or to study after the usual or expected time for leaving

suspend (v) to make someone leave their job or school for a short time, especially because they have broken the rules

sustainable (adj) able to continue without causing damage to the environment

take turns (v phr) if people take turns doing work, etc., they do it one after the other in order to share the work or play fairly

tedious (adj) something that is tedious continues for a long time and is not interesting

threatening (adj) if someone's behaviour is threatening, you believe they intend to harm you

tireless (adj) working very hard in a determined way without stopping

tournament (n) a competition in which players compete against each other in a series of games until there is one winner

turn up (phr v) to arrive at a place, especially in a way that is unexpected

upbringing (n) the way your parents care for you and teach you to behave when you are growing up

vampire (n) in stories, a dead person that sucks people's blood by biting their necks

worse off (adv) in a worse situation or having less money

Unit 4

advent (n) the time when something first begins to be widely used

badger (n) an animal which has black and white fur, lives in holes in the ground, and is active at night

baldly (adv) in a way that is true but makes no attempt to be polite

baseline (n) a standard measurement or fact against which other measurements or facts are compared, especially in medicine or science

biosphere (n) the part of the world in which animals, plants, etc. can live

black market (n) a system by which people illegally buy and sell foreign money, goods that are difficult to obtain

blistering (adj) very hot

blockage (n) something that is stopping movement in a narrow place

boil down to (phr v) if a long statement, argument, etc. boils down to a single statement, that statement is the main point or cause

border on (phr v) to be very close to being something extreme

bypass (v) to avoid obeying a rule, system or someone in an official position

catch (n) a quantity of fish that is caught at one time

CEO (n) Chief Executive Officer – the person with the most authority in a large company

coach (v) to teach a person or team the skills they need for a sport

collapsible (adj) something collapsible can be folded so that it uses less space

composite (n) something made up of different parts or materials

container (n) a very large metal box in which goods are packed to make it easy to lift or move them onto a ship or vehicle

core (n) the central part of the Earth or any other planet

cornerstone (n) something that is extremely important because everything else depends on it

cross over (phr v) if an entertainer crosses over from one area of entertainment to another, they become successful in the second one as well as the first

cull (v) to kill some animals of a group, usually the weakest ones, so that the size of the group does not increase too much

debunk (v) to show that an idea or belief is false

diligent (adj) someone who is diligent works hard and is careful and thorough

directory (n) a place in a computer where files or programs are organized

download (v) to move information or programs from a computer network to a small computer

draw on (phr v) to use information, experience, knowledge, or part of a supply of something for a particular purpose

drive (n) determination and energy to succeed

driver (n) one of the main things that influence something or cause it to make progress

environmentalist (n) someone who is concerned about protecting the environment

extrinsic (adj) coming from outside or not directly relating to something

fibreglass (n) a light material made from small glass threads pressed together, used for making sports cars, motor boats, etc.

foster (v) to help a skill, feeling, idea, etc. develop over a period of time

guru (n) someone who knows a lot about a particular subject, and gives advice to other people

habitat (n) the natural home of a plant or animal

haven (n) a place where people or animals can live peacefully or go to in order to be safe

holistic (adj) considering a person or thing as a whole, rather than as separate parts

hunch (n) if you have a hunch that something is true or will happen, you feel that it is true or will happen

incentive (n) something that encourages you to work harder, start a new activity, etc.

ingestion (n) taking food or other substances into your body

inkjet printer (n) a printer that uses very small jets to blow ink onto paper to form letter, numbers, etc.

intact (adj) not broken, damaged or spoiled

interlock (v) if two or more things interlock, or if they are interlocked, they fit firmly together

intrinsic (adj) being part of the nature or character of someone or something

invasive (adj) spreading quickly and difficult to stop

ivory (n) the hard, smooth, yellowish-white substance from the tusks of an elephant

lavish (adj) large, impressive or expensive

lead-in (n) remarks made by someone to introduce a radio or television show

limestone (n) a type of rock that contains calcium

lure (v) to persuade someone to do something, especially something wrong or dangerous, by making it seem attractive or exciting

molten (adj) molten metal or rock has been made into a liquid by being heated to a very high temperature

offset (adj) relating to a method of printing in which ink is put onto rollers and then the paper passes between the rollers

outsource (v) to arrange for someone outside a company to do work or provide goods for that company

pachyderm (n) an animal with thick skin, such as an elephant

pass up (phr v) to not make use of a chance to do something

performance-related pay (n) money that you earn for your work, which is increased if you do your work very well

perpetrator (n) someone who does something morally wrong or illegal

pesticide (n) a chemical substance used to kill insects and small animals that destroy crops

pharmaceutical (adj) relating to the production of drugs and medicines

plateau (n) a large area of flat land that is higher than the land around it

poach (v) to illegally catch or shoot animals, birds or fish, especially on private land without permission

porpoise (n) a sea animal that looks similar to a dolphin and breathes air

print run (n) the number of books or magazines that are printed at the same time

proliferate (v) if something proliferates, it increases quickly and spreads to many different places

proxy (n) if you do something by proxy, you arrange for someone else to do it for you

pundit (n) someone who is often asked to give their opinion publicly of a situation or subject

relief (n) a way of decorating wood, stone, etc. with a shape or figure that is raised above the surface, or the decoration itself

reluctant (adj) slow and unwilling

remote (adj) far from towns or other places where people live

remuneration (n) the pay you give someone for something they have done for you

sap (n) the watery substance that carries food through a plant

shareholder (n) someone who owns shares in a company or business

shift (v) to move from one place or position to another, or make something do this

shot (n) a small amount of coffee or a strong alcoholic drink

shun (v) to deliberately avoid someone or something

squatter (n) someone who lives in an empty building or on a piece of land without permission and without paying rent

stakeholder (n) someone who has invested money into something or who has some important connection with it, and is therefore affected by its success or failure

stocks (n pl) the total value of all of a company's shares

subsist (v) to stay alive when you only have small amounts of food or money

toner (n) a type of ink that is used in machines that print or copy documents

touch screen (n) a type of computer screen that you touch in order to tell the computer what to do or to get information

trash (v) to destroy something completely, either deliberately or by using it too much

tsunami (n) a tidal wave

tuna (n) a large sea fish caught for food

update (n) the most recent news or information about something

upload (v) if information, a computer program, etc. uploads, or if you upload it, you move it from a small computer to a computer network so that other people can see it or use it

wildebeest (n) a large Southern African animal with a tail and curved horns

wilderness (n) a large area of land that has never been developed or farmed

wildlife (n) animals and plants growing in natural conditions

wipe out (phr v) to destroy, remove or get rid of something completely

Unit 5

bonanza (n) a lucky or successful situation where people can make a lot of money

boost (v) to increase or improve something and make it more successful

burst (n) a sudden short effort or increase in activity

circumvent (v) to avoid a problem or rule that restricts you, especially in a clever or dishonest way – used to show disapproval

coalface (n) place where the real work is done, not just talked about

community of interest (n) a group of people who share a common interest or passion. They exchange ideas, but may know (or care) little about each other outside of this area

consultancy (n) a company that gives advice on a particular subject; advice that a company is paid to prepare

cult (n) an extreme religious group that is not part of an established religion or a group of people who are interested in a particular thing

cyberspace (n) the connections between computers in different places, considered as a real place, where information, messages, etc. exist

double-edged sword (n) something that seems to be good but can have a bad effect

downturn (n) a period or process in which business activity, production, etc. is reduced and conditions become worse

drawback (n) a disadvantage of a situation, plan, product, etc.

eligibility (n) the ability or right to do something because you have the right qualifications, are the right age, etc.

endorsement (n) a public statement or action showing that you support someone or something

entrepreneur (n) someone who starts a new business or arranges business deals in order to make money, often in a way that involves financial risks

ethical (adj) morally good or correct; relating to the principles of what is right and wrong

fabric (n) the basic structure of a building, organization, story, etc.

fertiliser (n) a substance that is put on the soil to make plants grow

forgo (v) to not do or have something pleasant or enjoyable

forum (n) a group of computer users who are interested in a particular subject and discuss it using email or the Internet

gadget (n) a small, useful and cleverly-designed machine or tool

get through (phr v) to be successful in reaching a place

hamper (v) to make it difficult for someone to do something

hold out (phr v) to think or say that something is possible or likely to happen, especially something good

hold to account (v phr) to say that someone is responsible for something

host (n) a large number of people or things

hotbed (n) a place where a lot of a particular activity, especially bad or violent activity, happens

indispensable (adj) someone or something that is indispensable is so important or useful that it is impossible to manage without them

in-house (adj) working within a company or organization

insight (n) a sudden clear understanding of something or part of something, especially a complicated situation or idea

insurmountable (adj) an insurmountable difficulty or problem is too large or difficult to deal with

lucrative (adj) a job or activity that is lucrative lets you earn a lot of money

Luddite (n) someone who is opposed to using modern machines and methods

malnutrition (n) when someone becomes ill or weak because they have not eaten enough good food

MBA (n) Master of Business Administration – a university degree in the skills needed to be in charge of a business that you can get after your first degree. A person who has this is called an MBA

megastar (n) a very famous singer or actor

notion (n) an idea, belief or opinion

overarching (adj) including or influencing every part of something

parchment (n) thick, yellow-white writing paper, sometimes used for official documents

piracy (n) the crime of illegally copying and selling books, tapes, videos, computer programs, etc.

prestigious (adj) admired as one of the best and most important

quote (n) a statement of how much it will probably cost to build or repair something, or do some other work

remedial (adj) intended to improve something that is wrong

remit (n) the particular piece of work that someone has been officially asked to deal with

ringing endorsement (n) a statement that is made with a lot of force in support of something

run (n) a continuous series of performances of a play, film, etc. in the same place

scoop (n) an important or exciting news story that is printed in one newspaper or shown on one television station before any of the others know about it

scrabble (v) to try to find or do something very quickly, usually by moving your hands and feet in an uncontrolled way

set store by (v phr) consider something to be very important

shipping (n) the delivery of goods, especially by ship

shortcoming (n) a fault or weakness that makes someone less successful or effective than they should be

smallholder (n) someone who has a piece of land used for farming, that is smaller than an ordinary farm

stalwart (n) someone who is very loyal to a particular organization or set of ideas, and works hard for them

stigma (n) a strong feeling in society that being in a particular situation or having a particular illness is something to be ashamed of

succumb to (phr v) to stop opposing someone or something that is stronger than you, and allow them to take control; if you succumb to an illness, you become very ill or die of it

takeover (n) when one company takes control of another by buying more than half its shares

technophobe (n) someone who does not like modern machines, such as computers, and would prefer to live without them

thrive (v) to become very successful or very strong and healthy

trust (n) an organization or group that has control over money that will be used to help someone else

uncompromising (adj) unwilling to change your opinions or intentions

underwrite (v) to support an activity, business plan, etc. with money and to take financial responsibility for it if it fails

untenable (adj) an untenable situation has become so difficult that it is impossible to continue

upmarket (adj) designed for or used by people who have a lot of money

virtual (adj) made, done, seen, etc. on the Internet or on a computer, rather than in the real world

wake (n) if something, especially something bad, happens in the wake of an event, it happens afterwards and usually as a result of it